Adam Ford is the founder of DIG International, which has been entrusted with archaeological investigations of some of the most historically significant sites in Australia. These include the location of Ann Jones's original hotel at Glenrowan, where Ned Kelly made his last stand against the police; Melbourne's historic Pentridge Prison; and the Dirk Hartog Island campsite of survivors of the shipwrecked French whaler *Persévérant*.

MY LIFE IN RUINS

MY LIFE IN RUINS

FROM PETRA TO GLENROWAN MY ADVENTURES AND MISADVENTURES IN ARCHAEOLOGY

ADAM FORD

ABC
Books

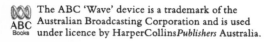 The ABC 'Wave' device is a trademark of the
Australian Broadcasting Corporation and is used
under licence by HarperCollins*Publishers* Australia.

First published in Australia in 2015
by HarperCollins*Publishers* Australia Pty Limited
ABN 36 009 913 517
harpercollins.com.au

HarperCollins*Publishers*
Level 13, 201 Elizabeth Street, Sydney NSW 2000, Australia
Unit D1, 63 Apollo Drive, Rosedale, Auckland 0632, New Zealand
A 53, Sector 57, Noida, UP, India
1 London Bridge Street, London, SE1 9GF, United Kingdom
2 Bloor Street East, 20th floor, Toronto, Ontario M4W 1A8, Canada
195 Broadway, New York NY 10007, USA

National Library of Australia cataloguing-in-publication entry:

Ford, Adam, author.
  My life in ruins / Adam Ford.
  ISBN: 978 0 7333 3319 4 (paperback)
  ISBN: 978 1 4607 0246 8 (ebook – epub)
  Subjects: Ford, Adam.
  Who's been sleeping in my house (Television program)
  Archaeologists – Australia.
  Excavations (Archaeology) – Australia.
  Historic sites – Australia.
  Other Creators/Contributors:
  Australian Broadcasting Corporation.
930.1092

Cover design by HarperCollins Design Studio
Front cover image: courtesy Australian Broadcasting Corporation
Back cover image: author's collection
Picture section images: *Who's Been Sleeping in My House* production photographs courtesy
Joined Up Films; unless otherwise indicated, all remaining photographs author's collection
Typeset in Baskerville MT by Kirby Jones
Printed and bound in Australia by Griffin Press
The papers used by HarperCollins in the manufacture of this book are a natural, recyclable
product made from wood grown in sustainable plantation forests. The fibre source and
manufacturing processes meet recognised international environmental standards, and carry
certification.

To the extraordinary IT
and the gorgeous Mixed Grills

CONTENTS

OF BONY FINGERS, BIPEDALISM AND BACK STORIES

The History of every major Galactic Civilisation tends to pass through three distinct and recognisable phases, those of Survival, Inquiry and Sophistication, otherwise known as the How, Why and Where phases. For instance, the first phase is characterised by the question, 'How can we eat?' The second by the question, 'Why do we eat?' And the third by the question, 'Where shall we have lunch?'

Douglas Adams, *The Hitchhiker's Guide to the Galaxy*, 1981

I work in the past and with people generally lacking in flesh, so sometimes I am a little slow at picking up on the subtle indicators of people's moods. But I could recognise an angry person when I saw one and I was looking at one now advancing across the archaeological dig site towards me, with a gun, a police uniform and, most worryingly, mirrored sunglasses.

'Hello, officer,' I said.

He stopped uncomfortably close to me. 'Is that yours?' he said, pointing at my old green Land Rover.

'Err ... yes it is.'

'It's parked illegally. Move it before I give you a ticket.' He hadn't turned his head during this brief conversation and I was drawn to the distorted and nervous reflection that stared back at me from his sunglasses.

I apologised, said I had no idea I couldn't park there and would move it immediately. I started patting my pockets for my keys.

He stepped in closer until his face was inches from mine. 'Just watch yourself, okay? We don't fucking like Ned Kelly, all right? He's a cop killer.'

I didn't know what to say so I didn't say anything, just nodded slightly.

With that he turned and stalked off, pausing to look at his now muddy shoes. He threw me a parting grimace before jabbing a finger at the Land Rover and getting into his patrol car.

I slowly breathed out and looked across the vacant block where the team had just started to clear away some of the surface vegetation. It was early June 2008, I was four hours into digging the most famous historical site in Australia, and the local police had just made it very clear that we weren't welcome in town.

That town was Glenrowan and the vacant block was the location of Ann Jones's inn, the site of the famous siege and gun battle between the Kelly Gang and the Victorian colonial police on 28 June 1880. In late 2007 I had been commissioned by the government to excavate the inn site. This would be the first occasion anyone had archaeologically investigated the famous landmark. By this time I had over fifteen years' experience as an archaeologist on digs around the world, from beachfront campsites in Barbados to desert villages in Jordan, from Cold War bunkers in the UK to remote islands off the west coast of Australia. It was an unbelievable honour to be trusted with the dig, and even though I'd been directing excavations for almost ten years, this one was a daunting task.

This excavation was the culmination of my career to that point. After all, who gets to dig into a legend? I certainly didn't see that in my future when I first became interested in archaeology. Mind you I was quite young.

*

I was seven when a dead monk called Alphonse pointed my career path out to me.

It was during the summer of 1977, 10 July to be precise, about eleven o'clock in the morning. Up to this point the British summer had run to script and had therefore been dreadfully disappointing. The previous year, the fabled summer of '76, was the hottest since records began for our typically mild, damp islands. For fifteen consecutive days, between 23 June and 7 July, the thermometer had topped thirty-two degrees Celsius, and my hazy recollection is one of a golden time, not least because it was the last summer that the whole family would be together. Debbie, my older sister, headed to university in the autumn of that year to study archaeology.

The summer of '77, however, was cool and dull. The chart music – avidly followed in the Ford household – was, with the exception of Donna Summer's 'I Feel Love', just terrible. And I was bored. Bored, bored, bored, bored, bored. I'm seven years younger than my nearest sibling, Matt, and eleven and twelve years younger that my eldest brother, Mark, and sister, Debbie, respectively. That meant in 1977 I played a lot of toy soldiers in the back yard while the others explored the worlds of dates, pubs and punk rock.

When my parents announced that they were taking me to visit Debbie on an archaeological dig, I was in the back seat of the Ford Zephyr before they had finished cutting the sandwiches. Sandwiches were a must on any Ford family road trip, no matter how short. Usually corned beef (from the can that opened with a key and was designed to inflict nasty gashes on anyone within a couple of feet of it) and Branston pickle, or cheese and Marmite (a British spread – saltier than Lot after he decided to have one last look over his shoulder at home and with the consistency of road tar, but totally delicious). Always accompanied by a tartan Thermos of steaming hot tea.

Mum and Dad, bless them, had taken Debbie's unusual and last-minute degree choice in their stride. A little more than a year before, she had been heading to medical school, but a change of heart meant that we found her six feet down a muddy, occupied grave in the grounds of Lichfield Cathedral, wearing a pair of oversized grey dungarees and a very big smile.

By and large, archaeologists aren't a particularly intimidating bunch of people, but this was the '70s and I remember a bewildering amount of hair and lurid, chunky knitwear floating about the site. Awkward and shy was my usual modus operandi around adults (with or without lots of hair) and so, after a blushing introduction to Debbie's muddy friends, I scampered off. My parents picked their way across the site, trailing behind the tousled head of Martin Carver, the site director and prominent British archaeologist, while he expounded on medieval monastic life.

I really hadn't the foggiest what was going on or what my sister was doing. She had left for university as a straight-A student with pigtails and a backpack, to return only a few months later wearing black make-up and a safety pin through her ear, listening to bands called The Slits and Sham 69 and saying 'Bog off' all the time. And now she was digging holes in the ground and finding skeletons. To a young lad like me, her whole transformation was unnerving but darkly thrilling.

I climbed to the top of the largest heap of dirt that had been cast up next to the trenches and was sitting there surveying the whole dig when I looked down between my feet and saw a grubby bone seemingly pointing directly at me out of the ground.

I picked it up and turned it over in my hands, rubbing the sticky wet clay off its grey surface. It was small; maybe a couple of centimetres long. Of course I had no knowledge of such things back then, but I immediately decided that it was a human bone. The thought fired my imagination and scared me at the same time, and sent me tumbling down the spoil heap in a dead sprint towards Debbie, who was talking with Mum and Dad and the director. I stopped in the middle of them and held out my hand with the bone lying in my palm. Mum clucked at me, Debbie smiled and asked what I'd been up to, and the director swept up the bone and, after a quick glance, asked me where I'd found this treasure.

'Up there,' I said, pointing at the crest of the spoil heap.

'Oh,' muttered Martin, and regarded the odd assortment of hippies kneeling down in the dirt, scraping away with their trowels. He scowled. 'Right, well what you have there, son, is an intermediate phalanx.'

I blinked and Mum said, 'A finger bone? Really?'

Debbie looked quite abashed. I had found part of a finger of a monk buried in the grounds of the cathedral more than 500 years ago, and I'd picked it up on the spoil heap, which meant that someone had missed it while excavating one of the burials. I now know, of course, that this was a bit of a boo-boo and the reason both Martin and my sister looked a little embarrassed.

I didn't take any notice of this at the time. I had found something important and gruesome and human. I was ecstatic and, eager to discover more, hared back up the spoil heap, scanning the lumpy surface for more artefacts. Atop the summit, I stopped and looked around and tried to imagine what everything would have looked like when my finger bone was alive and attached to a monk. But I couldn't. I didn't have the knowledge to put that finger back where it came from and imagine what it had done five centuries before. Mind you, on reflection, that's probably just as well.

It was there and then, standing on a mound of mud, that I decided I was going to become an archaeologist, though I didn't really know what one was, definitely couldn't spell it and was deeply unsure about the huge jumpers.

*

Archaeology is an ungainly word. Its anachronistic spelling makes it overly burdened with vowels, unless you are American (a nation that takes to superfluous vowels with an ax), in which case you are saved from the second 'a'. And unless you happen to be an Ancient Greek scholar or a fan of Indiana Jones, its meaning doesn't immediately jump out at you. When you see the titles shop assistant, doctor, builder you know what those people do, but archaeology …

So for the benefit of those who haven't studied ancient languages, or who aren't archaeologists, here's a bit of background. The science of archaeology is the study of the human past through the investigation and analysis of the physical evidence left behind. The word comes from the Greek *arkhaios*, meaning 'ancient', and *logia*, meaning 'the study of'.

Fundamentally, the study of archaeology is the study of our back story.

There a couple of things that archaeologists are not concerned with. We don't do dinosaurs. They died out about sixty million years before the earliest proto-human apes appeared. Dinosaurs are studied and excavated by palaeontologists (more vowels), usually with dynamite. And the other is gold, which is the focus of geologists, South Africans and pirates. Mind you, the discovery of a golden dinosaur would be certain to pique the interest of the most stuffy archaeologist. Those aside, archaeology is a vast subject that incorporates a large number of sub-specialties such as field excavators, artefact specialists and those that look at the remains of plants (palaeoethnobotanists) and animals (zooarchaeologists) that humans used. All these have one common focus, us.

Humans, as you may know, are primates. (Regarding the creation versus evolution discussion, I subscribe to the evidence-based interpretation of what's around us. I'm yet to see evidence to prove the creation model and I haven't seen convincing evidence to disprove evolution. Mind you, I would be deliriously happy to be proved wrong. To find out that all this stuff I've been digging up was put there as elaborate set dressing would be beyond cool.) So modern humans are the latest version of a group of primates or apes that can be distinguished from our cousins – the gibbons, chimpanzees, orangutans and gorillas – by bipedalism, or standing on two legs in an upright posture. All apes and most monkeys have limited movement on their hind legs, but that is not the same as bipedalism.

The current thought is that this physical development in our ancestors almost four million years ago directly caused, or significantly contributed to, the other startling physiological and mental developments that have made us the most successful, clever, adaptable and odd animal on the planet.

But why in the dim and distant past our ancestors decided to stand up is one of the greatest mysteries on earth. You see, bipedalism isn't the most obvious evolutionary step. Moving around on two legs requires an incredible number of muscle adjustments to keep us upright, which uses a significant amount of brain power. In those early days, hominids (the term used for not quite human bipedal apes) didn't have a hell of a lot of brain matter. It's quite possible they couldn't walk and talk at the same time …

This evolutionary change is thought to have occurred in the savannah lands of Sub-Saharan Africa, where knowing when to run, and run bloody quickly, was pretty useful for survival. But bipedalism didn't make us quicker. Chimpanzees, our nearest genetic relatives, can average forty shambling kilometres an hour over a short distance using an awkward but efficient combination of rear legs and knuckles. That might put them on the podium for the hundred-metre sprint at the Olympics. In fact, pretty much every other animal on the African plain could outrun us without getting out of breath.

So why have we developed into an animal that isn't quick, isn't particularly strong, has a patchy (in my case very patchy) fur coat that doesn't keep us warm or cool or protect us from the burning sun, and doesn't have a bite that's going to keep any predator up at night? It's possible, of course, that we are a terrible mistake and that hominids should have gone the way of the dodo millions of years ago. Indeed, there are scores of examples where animals have been painted into evolutionary corners.

The thing is, no one really has an answer and some of the greatest minds in medicine and physical anthropology have been thinking about it for over seventy years. One of the most popular theories for both development of bipedalism and hominid survival is that, while our early ancestors were scavengers and opportunist hunters, predominantly they were gatherers. When the forest habitat became sparser and dryer as the world's climate changed, food became less plentiful and increased effort was required to gain the calories needed to survive and thrive. When food is plentiful and always close by, in tropical forests for instance, there is no need to carry it away from its source, apart from perhaps to feed young or pregnant and nursing females. But out on the savannah, where fruit or seeds or ground roots and tubers are less abundant, the ability to carry food in freed-up hands may have become an advantage.

When not gainfully employed in carrying food, the free hands then started using objects as rudimentary tools. Hominids could use sticks to dig up tubers and break into termite mounds, to split open rotting trees to get at the grubs, to knock down bees' nests, hit tasty animals and fend off ones with big teeth. Then, perhaps in frustration at missing a particularly flighty gazelle, our hominid threw his stick after the retreating animal and by luck hit it. He added a point to the stick to pierce the sides of larger animals, then some bright spark put a sharp stone on its end that worked better. Someone realised that the sharp stone could be used independently of the stick to cut up the carcass of the animal caught with the stick, and dinner could be brought home. It was noticed that some stones worked better than others and it was worth caching these types and perhaps going a long way to collect them.

To spread the information about these inventions, language that others could understand became useful. And all of a sudden, an individual was not just reliant on the capacity of one brain and the luck of stumbling on solutions to problems alone, but could use amassed knowledge and experience. This saw the pace of hominid development increase exponentially. And throughout all this increased dexterity and industry, hominids became smarter and their brains became larger.

But this remarkable evolution isn't something that stopped when modern humans appeared on the scene about 200,000 years ago. It is charging ahead right now, except – for the first time in our planet's history – evolution is getting a helping hand by the very organism that it is changing. Science, medicine and communications and the countless other inventions of our world are changing us in ways that Mother Nature could never dream about.

The exploration of the lives led by countless people who I will never meet, but on whose shoulders we now stand, has been my life's work. It's been anything but a dull career and has taken me to amazing parts of the world. None more so than my first overseas dig.

OF MAOIST GUERRILLAS, SHALLOW GRAVES AND BOB MARLEY

Archaeology is the search for fact ... not truth. If it's truth you're looking for, Dr Tyree's philosophy class is right down the hall. So forget any ideas you've got about lost cities, exotic travel and digging up the world. We don't follow maps to buried treasure, and 'X' never, ever marks the spot ...

Indiana Jones, *Raiders of the Lost Ark*, 1981

The Sendero Luminoso (Shining Path) are your garden variety Maoist guerrilla outfit who, contrary to their spouting about being 'of the people' and 'fighting for the people', killed loads of Peruvians and imprisoned many more in forced labour camps. Typically, at the first whiff of the Peruvian authorities closing in, they would mumble something about checking to see if they had left the gas on and would abandon their sympathisers to suffer the inevitable bloody reprisals. Active since 1980, the Shining Path have the stated aim of turning the country into a 'new democratic' state functioning as a 'dictatorship of the people'. They are still active, particularly in the more remote Andean communities, but are a shadow of their former selves since the arrest of their founder and leader, Abimael Guzmán, in the early 1990s.

All in all, they're the usual band of thugs armed to the teeth with banal rhetoric and AK-47 assault rifles who 'just want to make the world a better place'. That is, a better place for themselves and a thoroughly miserable place for everyone else. Ordinarily, my egocentric teenage self wouldn't have given two hoots, but the Shining Path had inadvertently made my life miserable too (although to a vastly lesser degree when compared to the average Andean peasant).

After my revelatory incident with the medieval monk's digit (now, behave), I spent the next ten years digging up my back yard and reading everything I could find about the past. Mayfield, my childhood home, was a beautiful two-storied Georgian cottage probably built towards the end of the eighteenth century. Like all houses built before council refuse collection, which didn't become widespread in the UK until after the Second World War, the back yard of my house had been used to dispose of household rubbish. Odd bits of broken glass and pottery regularly surfaced in the garden and were snatched up by my grubby hands, cleaned and squirrelled away in shoeboxes and old tobacco tins. These mundane fragments opened a window onto a past that, despite being only two hundred years before, was a completely different time to mine. Back then my house sat within farmland on the edge of the Mordor-esque landscape that was the industrial 'Black Country' of the English Midlands. It was called the Black Country due to the layer of coal dust and soot that coated the countryside and the people who toiled in the many mines and foundries. The reference to Mordor is not my literary comparison but JRR Tolkien's take on the despoiling of his native surrounds. Tolkien grew up in the Midlands at a time when the last vestiges of the English rural idyll gave way to the noise, smoke and fire of a revolution that had started in the cotton mills of Lancashire and exploded across the Black Country.

Tolkien's childhood coincided with the end of a medieval way of life that had changed little for hundreds of years. It's amazing to think of this now, but less than one hundred and fifty years ago fields were worked by men and horses, cows were milked by hand, there were no cars or trucks, no planes in the sky, no concrete or bitumen, electricity pylons or television. Life moved to the slow beat of the seasons and one's thoughts were interrupted only by the crow of a rooster or the whir and clack of farm machinery worked by actual horsepower of the four-legged variety.

As I turned the fragments of dinner plates and curious bottles over in my hands, I thought that this past was a lot less complicated and a lot more adventurous than the existence I was living at the time. The Midlands that I inhabited in my youth were safe and comfortable and, being the 1970s, mostly beige and made of synthetic fibres that snagged if brushed against anything rougher than a billiard ball.

Around the same time that I was making a mess of the back garden, my sister, Debbie, was working on an archaeological project in Peru. From the valleys below the world-famous Machu Picchu ruins, she sent home letters from which sprang stories that were terrifyingly seductive. In tiny lettering that filled every space on the flimsy blue airmail paper, she talked about strange ancient ruins and jungles and poor people and mountains and death and illness and danger and robbery and crazy journeys in overcrowded buses along precipitous roads. She described all this in a wonderfully rich way that grabbed me by the collar from where I read cross-legged in front of the gas fire and pulled me into the steamy forests, colourful markets and dizzy valleys of South America. Not only did the stories of the past seem exciting, but it appeared that being an archaeologist in pursuit of those stories was a wild adventure too.

As I entered my teens, I pursued the past with greater intent. I badgered my parents to take me to castles and hill forts, and when I was old enough, I volunteered on archaeological digs during the summer holidays. There was no question that I was going to go to university to study archaeology, and I was over the moon when I got accepted into the Institute of Archaeology, at University College London.

The institute encouraged students to gain as much digging experience as possible both on UK excavations and digs around the world. So with my sister's stories still swirling around in my head, I signed up to an excavation in Peru. I'd never been overseas before and I was beyond excited. But a week before I was due to fly out of London on my very own adventure, the Shining Path murdered a British tourist on the Inca Trail only a few miles from the dig and the project was cancelled at the last moment. I was devastated.

*

Two rather frantic weeks and a lot of phone calls later, I stood in the middle of the busy concourse of Grantley Adams Airport with my rucksack stuck to my back, my sweaty shirt clinging to my body and an overwhelming, sickening realisation that I was completely and utterly useless.

Ahead of me was a throng of people chatting excitedly about their holiday plans in front of a line of cubicles. Passport control. The invisible but nonetheless well-guarded barrier between the strange no-man's-land of international airspace and the sovereign island country of Barbados. I was an inexperienced traveller, and while I had managed to book a ticket on a plane that actually went to Barbados it struck me, as I shuffled forward in the queue, that I had failed to organise anything else.

This oversight was received with a serious look at passport control. 'What is the purpose of your visit to Barbados?'

I explained that I was to join an archaeological expedition.

'Where?'

I didn't know where.

'Who for?'

'The Institute of Archaeology,' I said. 'In London.'

'Who's your contact here in Barbados?'

I didn't know.

'How long do you intend to stay?'

I didn't know that either.

'Where are you going to stay during the dig?'

I wasn't sure.

'When is the dig going to start?'

I brightened up. 'About a month from now,' I said. The only flight I could get at such short notice was a whole month before the dig and until that moment it hadn't occurred to me that this could be a problem.

'Where are you going to stay until this dig starts and what are you going to do?'

I looked down like a naughty child.

It was at this point that I thought perhaps my parents' hands-off approach since I'd left school was a little too hands-off. These days, my wife, Inga, and I always check and double-check what our two girls are doing, where they are going and who they are with. Okay, so they aren't eighteen yet, but I'm pretty sure when that time comes and they are about to head overseas, we'll say more than, 'Have a nice time, dear.'

The passport officer looked at me.

I looked back at her.

She erupted into laughter. I must have presented a pathetic sight. A pale, sweaty youth with a scraggly beard, big backpack and not the slightest hint of a clue. She straightened her face and pointed at a wall of brochures. She told me to find a hotel and come back with the details.

That night I lay in a little hotel room somewhere in Bridgetown, the capital of Barbados, and panicked a bit. I was floored by the heat and humidity of the tropical night. The air was so thick I felt like I was breathing underwater. The noise of frogs chirping was so loud it made me laugh, and the smells that wafted in through the open window were strange and sweet but with the sickly edge of decomposition.

I'd spent an hour wandering the streets looking for the hotel. I'd only made two wrong turns and it wasn't such a long time, but it was enough to knock the 'cocky man of the world' stuffing out of me, and I contemplated the possibility that I might be homesick. I was so disappointed with myself. Some adventurer I was turning out to be. Would it be a record, becoming homesick after less than three hours in another country, albeit a very remote one?

Barbados is a tiny speck of land thirty-four kilometres long and only twenty-three kilometres at its widest point. Sitting somewhat alone in the western Atlantic Ocean, it's the most easterly of all the Caribbean islands, lying almost two hundred kilometres from its nearest neighbour, St Vincent. It was first described on a Spanish map, dated to 1511, as Los Barbudos, but the island was occupied for two thousand years prior to first European contact. These early colonisers are often called Amerindians, which is a contraction of the two words American Indian. Unfortunately, it's a term that neither describes the ethnicity nor the origin of these peoples. By the time the first Europeans made contact with the islanders of the region they were known as Caribs, from which the island chain and sea take their names.

When Captain John Powell landed in 1625 and claimed Barbados for King James I, he found the island uninhabited. There are a few possibilities to explain why no one was home. Powell may have been fibbing (not unheard of in expeditionary accounts, particularly if there is land up for grabs), Spanish and Portuguese raiding parties during the sixteenth century might have seized so many slaves that the population became unsustainable, or the island might have been abandoned for some reason before European contact. Whatever the case, Barbados after 1625 became an extremely important colony, and the wealth generated on this modest coral atoll fuelled the expansion of the British Empire and formation of the modern world.

I, on the other hand, had so little money that I needed to do something quickly. Another four nights paying peak holiday rates in the hotel would wipe me out. It was then I remembered that one of the team, Sandy, a second-year student at the institute, was a Barbadian national, and I vaguely recalled that her family was going to provide their beach house for the dig accommodation. Perhaps I could stay there until the dig started? The sensible thing would have been to note down her family's details before I flew, but I hadn't. I did remember her last name, Rogers, and so I phoned every Rogers in the local phone book until one responded positively to my strange question, 'Do you have a family member studying archaeology in London?'

A woman answered with the rich, broad, rolling accent of the Caribbean, and I was momentarily confused. I had always associated the West Indian accent with, well, West Indians, the black population of the Caribbean, but Sandy was white. Shamefully, I thought perhaps this woman was the housekeeper (did I think I was in *Gone with the bloody Wind?*). I explained my predicament and she was kind enough not to call me an idiot and to insist that I come to her house and she would sort it all out. With instructions on how to get to her house, I jumped on a bus and headed east to the suburb of Graeme Hall. Walking along the hot back roads, I marvelled at the tropical trees with boughs weighed down by limes and other fruit I didn't recognise. These draped over walls that were stained by mould and festooned with wandering vines like Christmas bunting. Graeme Hall seemed to be an old part of Bridgetown and had grand colonial-looking houses set back from the street. And the Rogers house was one of the grandest, situated to the north of a small quiet square that was formed by tall property walls and had a large shady tree growing from a small circular garden in the middle.

The house stood amid simple tropical gardens of lush grass and exotic trees from which hung, in great shaggy beards, the grey lichen-like growth that is thought to have given the island its name. As I mentioned, the Spanish named the island Los Barbudos, but where that name comes from is a mystery. A popular theory is that it is the Portuguese name for a beard and refers to the long wispy epiphytic plants that hang from the branches of the coastal trees.

The house was imposing, with plantation shutters across all the windows, which, when viewed while standing in the heat, invited the mind to imagine cool and peaceful spaces within. I pushed open the gate and before I could get to the front door, a tall, smiling woman in perhaps her fifties came quickly to meet me. She welcomed me in the same easygoing accent of the black Barbadians I had met over the previous few hours but she was as white as me – though not exactly, as I was translucent compared to her deeply tanned skin.

She introduced herself as Barbara and swept me inside, through what were indeed cool and serene rooms, all dark timber floors and wall panelling, into a bright family kitchen. Over a cooling fresh lime juice and soda, I explained who I was and how I'd ended up sitting in her kitchen. (Lime and soda, a first and an enduring favourite. In fact, if I had to choose a drink I could sip on for the rest of my life, barring all others, it would be fresh lime and soda.) I didn't think for a moment that I was going to impose on them other than perhaps to stay at their beach house until the team turned up.

So when Barbara said that I should stay with them, I didn't know what to say. I hadn't been looking forward to spending a month by myself but, hey, I was in paradise so I reckoned I could push through. I feebly tried to argue but she wouldn't have a word of it. She put me at my ease by reasoning that I was helping her out, as another young lad was staying with the family for the summer and I would be great company for him.

I was shown to a comfortable and homely room, given a fresh towel and told to forage for food and drink from the fridge while she headed out for an hour or two. Then she was gone and I was left alone in a beautiful old house in the Caribbean. Less than twenty-four hours after arriving without a clue, a place to stay or much money, I had landed on my feet. I have to admit this does sum up my life, and I am frequently surprised and humbled by the generosity and kindness of strangers.

The other visitor turned out to be a guy called Philippe, who was from Guadeloupe, a French Caribbean island to the north, and he was staying with the Rogers to improve his English. He was tall and tanned and good-looking, and while he was only a little younger than me, he seemed very young and innocent. He was a gentle fellow and funny, and I liked him.

Philippe and I were pretty much left to our own devices over the next three weeks. With his clean-living outlook and my slim wallet we stayed away from the distractions of the resorts and spent our days swimming, body surfing, playing beach tennis and generally 'liming' on the extraordinarily beautiful beaches along the south coast of the island. 'Liming' is a Barbadian term that means just hanging out, as limes hang from the trees. Worthing and Dover beaches (nothing like their British namesakes, nothing) were a short walk from the house, and we spent days on them living a life that up till then I could only have dreamed about. I got fit, I got a tan and Barbados seemed to me, at the tender age of nineteen, the most perfect place on earth.

When I was there, unemployment rates were almost zero, local telephone calls were free and for $1 the public buses would take you anywhere on the island. And these weren't ordinary public transport vehicles. They were more like wheeled subwoofers that happened to pick people up. I remember standing at a little tin bus stop on an empty stretch of road that cut through the rustling cover of sugar cane carpeting much of the island. The road snaked around the old plantation boundaries and so it disappeared to the left and right behind the scrappy curtains of cane. I began to hear a low hum, the broken and unmistakable rhythmic beat of reggae. As the music got louder I looked to see where it was coming from, but the road remained empty. Eventually, an old Toyota Coaster bus trundled into view and I was staggered at how loud the music was even though the vehicle was still a good couple of hundred metres away. When it stopped and the door snapped open, I was almost knocked back into the cane by the blast of the bass. Inside, the noise made my eyes water. Six little electric fans were directed at the overworked amplifier that sat on the dashboard next to the grinning bus driver, whose dreadlocks were crammed into a red, yellow and green woolly hat that poked up at a jaunty angle over the back of his seat. The bus was crowded with mostly cane-field workers who lived in the brightly painted villages that dotted the interior of the island. I sat next to a middle-aged woman who hooted with amusement at having such a hilarious thing as me beside her. Without warning, she threw an arm around me and pulled my head into her enormous bosom. There didn't appear to be any reason for this gesture, but the whole bus cracked up. I was held there for the count of ten, released briefly and then pushed back in, causing another round of merriment.

Anyone who lives in northern Europe will tell you that they can handle the rain and the cold quite cheerfully, but it's the overcast dull light, which sometimes lasts for weeks, that slowly pulls you down during the colder months. So the joyous sunshine of Barbados gave me more than a tan. It seemed to seep in, slowing me down, making me smile. I sloughed off some of the reserved and dour Englishness that is part national character and part reaction to the weather. It's difficult to describe the feeling. The closest I can think of is the light, liberating feeling you get when, after a long day on the road, you drop a heavy backpack to the ground.

Philippe and I stumbled through one idyllic day to another with beach trips perfectly balanced by parties, barbecues and raucous evenings at lively beach bars. Good grief, it was fantastic. This island life of mine reached a crescendo of wonderfulness with the annual Crop Over Festival. It's a harvest festival originating in 1688 to celebrate the end of the sugar-cane harvest in the days when cane was cut by hand, and all the cane cutters could at last stand up straight and work out the aches and pains with a bit of a party.

Actually, I was surprised to see that cane was still cut by hand. I would watch scores of people climb on and off buses swaddled in thick layers of cloth, no doubt to protect themselves from the sharp leaves of the cane. Mechanical cane cutters were common elsewhere at the time, so whether these guys cut cane in difficult-to-access locations or the old ways were maintained to continue full employment I don't know, but considering the amazing employment rate, I suspect the latter.

Over the centuries the Crop Over Festival had grown to be like a mardi gras, with vibrant competitions between bands and floats and parade troupes culminating in the Grand Kadooment or parade. Unlike the larger festivals in Rio de Janeiro or the great Crop Over in Trinidad, the Barbados festival maintained a local, family feel. The bands all took names that were easy to remember and easier to show support for. One band was called Red Plastic Bag, another White Plastic Bag. For the few weeks leading up to the festival, the rival bands were given airplay on the radio and people showed their affiliation by tying coloured shopping bags to their bikes and car aerials. The music was entirely calypso and, with the cascading bell-like sounds of steel drums and a strange syncopated beat, it fit perfectly with the weather and people but I found it impossible to dance to. Unfortunately, I couldn't help but try to dance to it, and I wince at the memory of waggling my arms and legs around, completely off-beat, like a pink eejit.

The Grand Kadooment at the end of the festival was a joyous experience with music playing and floats parading through the streets. It seemed that everyone on the island was in Bridgetown, dancing, blowing whistles, drinking rum and eating Barbados's national dish – macaroni cheese. I kid you not, the humble mac and cheese, so in and out of vogue in the hip eateries of the world. The Barbadian version is more like a solid pie that also incorporates chilli to give it a bit of a kick. It's delicious and if you are intrigued enough to try it, I've included a recipe at the end of the chapter. Easy. Relax.

Without exception, everyone I encountered, from the market store owners to bus drivers and police officers, were generous with their time and genuinely friendly in a very funny way. But none were as hilarious as the drug pushers who cruised the tourist beaches. There were two I remember, the Doctor and Mr Brown. The Doctor would weave his way towards you in board shorts and flip flops and holding a black briefcase. With a flourish, he would slip the catches of the briefcase and announce that he was the 'doctor of the beach' and had every cure you could need right there. Mr Brown described himself as 'Mr Brown, the handyman of town'. He would grin and say, 'I can fix anything,' and tap meaningfully at his shoulder bag.

Of course, my impression of Barbados as a tropical utopia is naive bollocks. The island's history is a story of the dirty, brutal and shameful reality of British colonialism. The black Barbadians are the descendants of the West African diaspora carried to the West Indies to work the sugar plantations from the seventeenth to nineteenth centuries. They arrived at Bridgetown on the second leg of a miserable triangular journey. Starting in the great ports of London, Bristol and Liverpool, slave ships travelled south with goods and tradable supplies. Once off-loaded at one of the numerous ports that dotted the 'Slave Coast' of the Bight of Benin, these ships were filled with a living cargo bound for the Americas. It is estimated that twelve million people landed in south, central and north America between the sixteenth and nineteenth centuries. Many more left Africa but didn't survive the crossing. The ships later returned to Britain packed to the gunwales with a precious cargo of sugar, cotton and tobacco.

The Swahili term *maafa* is often used to describe this trade. It means 'great disaster', and they're not bloody kidding. Barbados was Britain's first established colony in the Caribbean, but until the 1640s the population was predominantly white and male, and the economy based on tobacco, cotton, ginger and indigo. Indentured European labourers provided most of the intensive labour for tending these crops. But with the introduction of sugar in the middle of the seventeenth century, Barbados and the other British colony to its north, Jamaica, became the centres of the British slave trade in the Caribbean. Slavery was crucial to the development and profitability of sugar for the following 190 years until the trade was abolished in 1807 and slavery itself was outlawed in 1833. While we weren't going to be excavating a slave-era site, it was still essential for me and the rest of the dig crew to know the Barbadians' back story, to allow the dig to be undertaken with proper sensitivity to the locals.

Slavery has been around as long as there have been vicious sods willing to forego morality for profitability and force others to work for nothing. But in Barbados, slavery was codified into common law, no doubt to allow the aforementioned vicious sods to sleep soundly comforted by the fact that the Barbados Slave Code of 1661 legally allowed them to do entirely what they wished to any slave, including torture, corporal punishment and murder. However, the code did require the slave masters to provide one set of clothes per year per slave, so that was nice. Slavery is now outlawed in every country in the world, with the last one to come to the abolitionist table being Mauritania, ironically in West Africa, in 2007. Which is all well and good, but there are still an estimated thirty to forty million people enslaved around the world and the trade in humans is the third-largest illegal trade, estimated to be worth in excess of thirty-one billion US dollars per year.

It is incongruous that an inoffensive and seemingly benign luxury as sugar was the cause of such staggering misery and death. Sugar cane is an extremely fast-growing grass that is native to the tropics of South-East Asia and has been cultivated there for thousands of years. Through trade it spread to India, where it was refined for the first time in the first centuries AD, and then to Arabia and Persia where it was traded throughout the classical world of the Mediterranean. But until the sixteenth century, sugar was almost considered as precious and rare as a spice; as a boutique commodity to be enjoyed only by the wealthy and for a long time taken only as a medicine. Pedanius Dioscorides, the Greek physician and pharmacologist who wrote the influential pharmacopeia *De Materia Medica,* described sugar as 'a kind of coalesced honey called sakcharon found in reeds in India and Arabia Felix, similar in consistency to salt and brittle enough to be broken between the teeth like salt. It is good dissolved in water for intestines and stomach and taken as a drink to help a painful bladder and kidneys.'

Even though advances were made in sugar refinement, its cultivation required a lot of water and high temperatures, and harvesting and processing were hugely labour- and capital-intensive. So sugar remained as expensive as the rare spices such as mace and pepper. The word 'sugar' does not even appear in English texts until the late thirteenth century. The Portuguese introduction of sugar cane to Brazil at the beginning of the sixteenth century saw sugar prices slowly begin to fall. By the mid-1500s, there were almost three thousand sugar mills in Brazil and the north coast of South America. By the same time, small-scale production had started on the islands of Hispaniola (the island now divided into Haiti and the Dominican Republic), Jamaica and Cuba.

Early sugar production on Barbados was hampered by ignorance about the new crop and natural disaster. Barbados lies approximately thirteen degrees north of the equator, which is south of the common corridors of Atlantic hurricanes, but nonetheless sitting as it does on its own, the island gets battered by tropical storms, and every so often a hurricane swings south and gives it a slap.

But the sugar industry slowly established itself, helped by the fertile soils and the tenacity of the pioneer plantation owners, in particular James Drax, who brought both sugar cane and African slaves to the island in 1642. Sugar cane was harvested in the dry months between January and May, and once cut had to be hauled to the processing plant as quickly as possible. Cane was cut by hand and then transported on carts that ran on timber rails from the fields to the crushing mills. There it was fed into vertical rollers powered by teams of oxen. Later, wind power was used and the island bristled with over five hundred windmills.

The cane juice was then reduced through a complex series of boiling and skimming processes to create a thick, viscous fluid called molasses and a coarse, crystallised brown sugar called muscovado. The molasses was used for the manufacture of rum and for animal feed. (The oldest rum distillery in the world, Mount Gay, was established just outside Bridgetown in 1703 and still churns out great rum.) The muscovado was packed in barrels and shipped to Britain via the port at Bridgetown.

Within ten years of the introduction of the first sugar crops at the Drax plantation, ninety thousand acres of Barbados was under cane plantation and over eight thousand tons of sugar and molasses were being exported to British ports, with an estimated value of three million pounds. The British addiction to sugar and sweet foods increased dramatically over the next century. By the

1770s, Britain was importing almost a hundred thousand tons of sugar per year, a 1200 per cent increase on the previous century.

The construction of thousands of sugar mills throughout the sixteenth and early seventeenth centuries in South America and the Caribbean drove significant advances in technology and skill in the production of cogs, wheels, gears and machines. This technical knowhow helped kickstart the Industrial Revolution in the cotton mills of northern England. In addition, the wealth that sugar supplied through the plantations of Barbados fuelled the Revolution and British expansion throughout the eighteenth and nineteenth centuries.

At its height, the Atlantic sugar and cotton trade accounted for half of Britain's wealth. It is likely that without Britain's domination of the sugar industry in the Caribbean, the British Empire may never have eventuated. Which is amazing, or would be if it weren't for the fact that all this was made possible by the unimaginable depredations and misery of the slave trade.

We tut and suck through our teeth and shake our heads in disbelief that slavery occurred. We congratulate ourselves that the dreadful business is behind us. But it was clear to me that for the population of Barbados, both black and white, it is a very raw and painful past. During the dig we had to assure anxious and sometimes angry passers-by that we were not excavating a slave-era site.

Nevertheless, I do think that archaeology is well suited to explore these difficult stories. If carried out with strong community engagement and a clear objective approach, archaeological excavation can present the facts without apologetic or sentimental spin. It can provide visceral evidence without slanted interpretation or historical revisionism. I am firmly of the belief that people can make their own minds up, given the facts, and don't need someone to rewrite their ancestors' story for them. And that's one of the reasons I am so passionate about archaeology.

*

My holiday ended with the arrival of the dig team and the field director, Peter Drewett, one of my lecturers at the Institute of Archaeology in London. He had very graciously allowed me onto his dig at the last moment even though I was not his most favourite student. I had attended so few of his lectures in the first year that he did not recognise me when I turned up to the end-of-year exam. This wasn't my fault. Unfortunately his course, Introduction to the Prehistory of Britain, was at ten on a Tuesday morning, which was a terrible scheduling error. Monday night was the biggest night of the week at the student union, because that's when everyone caught up with their mates to find out what they had been up to on the weekend. Fridays were also pretty big. Saturdays, of course, go without saying. Wednesdays were the mid-week celebratory drinks. And Sundays …

I sadly had said goodbye to the Rogers, their house and to Philippe, who by now was well armed with a great variety of swearwords and Midland idioms and a liking for beer. As I mentioned before, the Rogers family had kindly given us their 'weekender' as accommodation during the dig. It was a small timber beach shack in the parish of St Philip to the north-east of Bridgetown on the Atlantic coast. The shack was pretty basic and way too small for all the team to sleep inside, but it had a huge verandah overlooking the road and most of us slept out there. It sat on its own on a dusty side road that led off the main island highway towards a small beach amusingly called Bottom Bay, one of the most beautiful beaches I have been to. Surrounded by twenty-metre-high cliffs, it was the quintessential tropical beach with swaying palm trees, snow-white sand and blue-green sea.

The only real downside to the shack were the hordes of unwanted guests in the shape of thumb-sized orange cockroaches. Now, the British Isles sit high up in the North Atlantic, much further north than you would think. For comparison, the most southerly land in Australia – excluding Southern Ocean islands – is the South East Cape of Tasmania at approximately forty-three degrees south of the equator. London is fifty-one degrees north. The northernmost point of the British Isles is the northern tip of the Isle of Unst, which lies at 60.8 degrees north of the equator. That's only six degrees off the Arctic Circle and on the same latitude as the southern cape of Greenland.

Most of the UK sits north of Newfoundland, and by rights, the country should be blanketed in snow and ice for half the year. The reason it's not is that it's bathed in the balmy waters of the Caribbean region, miraculously carried to UK shores by the Gulf Stream and North Atlantic Drift. While you couldn't honestly describe sea waters off the coast of the British Isles as warm, they are considerably warmer than would ordinarily be found at such high latitudes. The current crosses the Atlantic from the American north coast and drags with it air, warmed by the sea below, that carries a significant amount of moisture which it dumps on the first bit of land it drifts across: the British Isles.

This results in a group of islands that aren't particularly cold but are very wet. The reason I'm going on about the British climate – well, as a Brit I had to get a conversation about the weather in somewhere – is that this climate is not attractive to many large creepy crawlies. At least, none approaching the calibre of the cockroaches I encountered in Barbados. They were terrifying to us sunburnt Brits. They had enormously long mahogany-coloured antennae that constantly tap-tap-tapped around them as if they were searching for something, and I became convinced that that something was me. Going to the loo at night was a traumatic experience, as a revolting carpet of the little buggers would scatter on chittering legs when you switched on the light. They peeked out of cracks in the walls and hared across floors and surfaces like hundreds of wind-up toys. I grew to loathe them and began to develop a real phobia, to the point where I refused to sleep inside even in the wildest weather, when Atlantic squalls ushered the other team members indoors.

So you can only imagine my reaction when one morning I woke up with the feeling that someone was tugging at my top lip. I opened my sand-crusted eyes and saw to my horror two fine mahogany feelers waving around a centimetre in front of my eyelashes. Their owner was sitting across my mouth and chin and was eating the peeling skin from my sunburnt top lip. I remember the magnified munching sound in the brief moment before I went from lying down to running down the road shouting and waving my arms around. Since then, and I think not unreasonably, I have had a bit of an issue with cockroaches. Occasionally, I still wake up in a cold sweat about that incident.

While the other team members were desperate to soak up the sun, I was keen to get on with the dig. Because I had come on board late, I had not attended any of the project briefings and so had no idea what we were doing. Peter Drewett wasn't necessarily the most effusive communicator, so when we arrived at the site the first morning I still hadn't a clue and the site itself gave no obvious indications of what lay beneath the surface.

In the district of St Martins on the south-east coast of Barbados, Silver Sands is a small but beautiful beach that sits between two craggy outcrops of jagged coral and is backed by a small, well-kept foreshore park of close cropped grass under clumps of swaying coconut palms. There was a small car park with a path to a public toilet block, and to the north ran a shallow creek that was barred from the sea by a low sand dune. It was the discovery of artefacts eroding out of the bank of this creek that persuaded Peter to dig here. To the north of this rather stagnant water were the backs of small houses, out of which came a dozen or so curious locals to see what we were up to when we started unpacking the dig gear and measuring out the first trenches.

The excavation lasted for eight weeks and throughout that time we were always surrounded by between ten and twenty amiable locals. Archaeological excavation is a slow affair. Watching it proceed is like watching paint dry or grass grow, but our audience was content to sit around chatting among themselves and occasionally throwing a gentle quip or jibe at us.

Whereas historians look at written accounts, books, texts and art to piece together a story, archaeologists look at the fragmentary physical remains of the human past, whether they be skeletons (the most personal artefacts), remains of buildings or possessions, or even landscapes, if they have been altered by human activities. In order to discover evidence of the archaic activities of our ancestors, we dig holes in the ground, very slowly. The pace of excavations is not because we've got nothing better to do – although that's true of many of us – it is because archaeological excavation is an unrepeatable experiment. We only have one shot at digging a site, because as we dig a site we destroy it. So we carefully and methodically retrieve as much information as possible to mitigate the impact of its destruction. We record every feature, wall or pit. Every change in soil colour or texture and the exact location and nature of artefacts are noted down. We retrieve soil samples so that experts can analyse the tiny bones or enduring plant fragments such as pollen that might lie within them. Then all this data is analysed and interpreted, and hopefully enough pieces of the jigsaw survive to enable us to glimpse a little moment in time.

Silver Sands was one of the most idyllic site locations I have ever excavated at. The sea was thirty metres away, glittering through the trees at us. If we got too hot we would run in for a quick dip and return in dripping board shorts to continue digging. The trenches were in shade for most of the day and we were excavating through sand which, compared with the cloying clays of England, was bliss.

The excavation wasn't particularly complicated. The archaeological deposits of what appeared to be only a few short periods of occupation were shallow, but the remains were fascinating. Our efforts soon uncovered evidence of a small encampment, and from the distinctive artefacts it was concluded that almost a thousand years ago this little foreshore park had been home to a small group of people, perhaps a family.

Not much is known about the first islanders, but consensus among Caribbean archaeologists is that groups from the delta lands of the Orinoco River on the northern coast of Venezuela migrated north and first settled the islands of Trinidad and Tobago in the second and third centuries BC. These lie so close to the mouth of the Orinoco that the southern beaches of Trinidad are thick with the brown silt of the mighty river. From there it was a short hop to Grenada, St Vincent and the Grenadines, then further north to St Lucia and east to Barbados. Archaeological evidence shows that occupation of the Antilles and Windward Isles (the two archipelagos that make up the southern Caribbean Islands) happened in waves over the following fifteen hundred years.

It was not known if our group were migrants from the delta lands or island-born descendants. However, here on the banks of this small stream, the group set up home and did what people have done all over the world for thousands of years. They built shelters, caught and cooked stuff to eat, made tools and cooking vessels and pretty things to wear, and died, of course. We discovered that our group wanted to keep their nearest and dearest close even after death. Very close. Indeed, they were buried directly (less than twenty centimetres) under where the living would have cooked and eaten and camped. It seems a bit odd, but I suppose we do something similar by keeping pictures and mementos of our dearly departed. I'm not sure how I'd go with Granddad under the telly, though.

Excavating human remains is both a thrilling and a sombre affair. One of the field practices drummed into us as students on our early digs was appropriate behaviour and respectful management of human remains, no matter their age or condition. Barbados was my first experience of excavating a burial, and even though I have dug up many skeletons since, I still remember the first. Perhaps that's because it was still in possession of a thick head of hair, skin that could have done with a good moisturiser and a lot of other body bits that shouldn't have been there.

This very rarely happens. In most civilised societies, disposal of our dead is legislated and formalised in such a way as to ensure respect for the dearly departed while maintaining the health of those still breathing. There are areas set aside for burial of bodies, minimum depths that bodies are to be buried and recording protocols so that the person's last resting place is known. That means, apart from murderers attempting to cover up their crime, bodies are not usually buried outside of a cemetery.

So my first burial find was a mystery. Four skeletons had already been excavated at the Silver Sands site. They were distinctly fleshless and appeared to have been buried with care and affection. They were found with coral and shell jewellery and other ceremonial grave goods, including parrot fish skeletons, placed at their feet. They were laid in crouched positions either on their sides or on their backs with their knees brought up towards their chest. This position suggests that they were wrapped in a piece of cloth or matting.

I had watched with great interest and some jealousy as the more experienced team members recovered these skeletons. Depending on the condition of the bone, excavating a burial is one of the more difficult tasks on an archaeological dig. Often you are lying on your belly with your head down a hole. You are trying to remove soil from around the skeleton without moving the bones, but at the same time you want to expose as much of the skeleton as possible so that you can establish how the body was buried. In many instances the bone is so fragile that you have to record dimensions and any pertinent features such as bone disorders, pre-mortem breaks and damage before you attempt to lift the bones, because they can crumble to pieces. Due to the morbid curiosity factor with human remains, particularly skulls, all this has to be achieved before you leave the site for the day, because it's not unheard of for skulls to go missing overnight.

The life of a person is more than the sum of their bony parts. However, a lot can be learned from analysis of skeletal remains. Visual observation can show the gender, height and age as well as certain pathologies that affect the bones such as tuberculosis, osteoporosis and syphilis. The wear on teeth can suggest the nature of the individual's diet, and from the wear on joints you can infer the nature and extent of work performed.

As an example, my grandfather Alfred was born in the 1880s and was at the younger end of a family of fourteen. His father worked hard but the family was poor, and as soon as the older boys were able, they worked hard too. At the dinner table in a brutal hierarchy of necessity, the workers got the most nutritious food and the younger ones made do with cups of tea and bread and jam or some other vitamin-bereft stomach filler. As a result, young Alfred developed rickets, a disease caused by a lack of vitamin D in infancy, which typically causes bowing of the legs. Of course, his skeleton would show this significant deformation of his legs and one could infer the cause, as it is the most common ailment of the poor and malnourished.

In recent years, analysis of the chemical make-up of bone (carried out by osteoarchaeologists – yet more vowels) has given a greater understanding of the life story of individuals uncovered. The chemical signature of the bone can quite accurately identify where the person lived and what the main component of their diet was. Sometimes the skeleton can show how the person died. One of the most recent and famous examples of human skeletal analysis is that carried out on the remains of King Richard III.

Demonised by Shakespeare and in popular history, Richard is often referred to as the hunchback, which is an unkind description of someone with a pronounced curvature of the spine caused by a number of conditions, scoliosis being one of them. It wasn't known until last year, when Richard's body was discovered, whether this was just name-calling by his detractors or whether he did have an abnormal spinal curve. Unsurprisingly, none of his official portraits showed any deformity.

But the skeleton discovered under a council car park in Leicester, the original location of the Greyfriars priory church where Richard's body was supposedly taken, had a pronounced curvature of the spine. It was also of the right date, ascertained by conducting radiocarbon dating of the bone. Richard was killed in the Battle of Bosworth Field after leading a charge against Henry Tudor's army. Hacking away, he got to within a sword's length of Henry before being cut down in a violent melee.

The skeleton found under the car park showed clear signs of perimortem (at time of death) injuries consistent with the not-so-subtle nature of medieval battle. Eleven separate injuries were detected on the bone. There were cuts to the cheek and jaw bones consistent with being stabbed in the face. These would have stung but wouldn't have killed him. The fatal blows were at the back of the head. One, possibly caused by a halberd, a vicious long-handled axe, cleaved a fist-sized part of the skull away, exposing the brain. The other was a stab wound, probably caused by a sword, that entered the back of the skull with such force it damaged the inside of the cranium on the opposite side, passing right through the brain. These wounds were consistent with the accounts describing Richard's death.

The clincher was positive matching of the skeleton's mitochondrial DNA (passed directly along female lines) with a living descendant of Richard's cousin. It was an extraordinary discovery and an amazing piece of archaeological detective work.

Richard was more than just a monarch made glorious by that son of Stratford-upon-Avon. He was one of those pivotal characters in history. If he had won the battle – and it is argued that he would have won at Bosworth Field if one of his trusted knights hadn't switched sides, taking a sizeable number of his army with him – then it is probable that Henry Tudor would have been killed before his son Henry VIII was born. Richard would have produced an heir and England would have remained Catholic. Without Henry VIII there may never have been a Church of England nor the vast Anglican Communion and its estimated eighty million adherents.

Excavation of human remains can tell us a lot about the story of our past, either in a personal context, or in the case of Richard III, a global one. So when I started to discern the first shadowy outline of a grave-shaped soil feature under the swaying palm trees of Silver Sands beach, my heart beat a little quicker. The director, Peter, came and joined me but all of a sudden he stopped trowelling and frowned. I looked down and could see a clear line of crumbling timber and a couple of rusty screws in the pale sand in front of us.

I said, 'Is that a coffin?'

He looked around and shrugged. 'I don't see why it would be. This is public ground and nowhere near a church graveyard or cemetery.'

But with a few scrapes of a trowel, I uncovered the side of a head. The hair was brittle, and the skin was cracked and drawn tight across the eye sockets and cheekbones. The lower jaw had fallen open into a permanent and unsettling gape, and the sinew and tendons of the neck could be clearly seen, dry and taut.

It was a gruesome sight and it sat me back on my heels. Peter swore and quickly placed an upturned bucket over the image before our local audience could see it.

'Right,' he said, looking wide-eyed. 'That is a modern burial. Within the last fifty years is my guess, and I have no idea what it's doing here. But I do know one thing. We are not digging this area anymore and we are not going to mention this to anyone.'

I was bitterly disappointed that I couldn't continue exploring my first burial, but I understood his decision. In

Barbados, as in most countries, unexplained or suspicious deaths such as a modern burial in foreshore parkland must be reported to the police, who would then have to ascertain how the body got there and would refer the case to the coroner to establish an inquest. In this instance, it is likely that the dig would have been halted. We only had two more weeks left, and we would have kissed that all goodbye if we had notified the authorities.

So we left the mystery burial partially reburied and continued the dig around it. On the last day we 'discovered' the remains and dutifully notified the Barbadian police.

I never heard anything more about it. It didn't seem likely that it was a victim of murder. Who murders someone and then buys a coffin and buries them? Whatever the story behind the corpse, it seemed a little sad that someone was buried and forgotten. I think that is the sombre part of excavating human remains: they each represent a mini tragedy.

A few days after my discovery, me and a mate called 'Fucking Hell' Steve (he said 'fucking hell' all the time ... often starting a sentence with the phrase) were slowly excavating a skeleton. I say slowly because nine hundred years in the sand had made the old bone very friable. As usual, we had a local audience and on that day two old guys were lounging back in a couple of our wheelbarrows, chatting away.

One noticed what we were doing and said in the broadest West Indian accent, 'Who is dat den?'

'We don't know, but they probably lived here about nine hundred —'

I was cut off by the other, who cackled, 'I bet him is Jesus Christ!' He threw back his silver-haired head and laughed out loud at his own wit. We'd stopped digging at this point, as had the other team members.

The other old guy, not to be out done, said, 'No man, dat dare is Bob Marley dem digging up!'

They both fell back into their barrows, gasping with mirth. With a whoop the grey-haired one stopped laughing suddenly, looked at the skeleton and then at his friend in shocked disbelief and said, 'But Bob Marley *is* Jesus Christ!' and that was both of them and us in fits of laugher for about twenty minutes.

It was that kind of dig.

The archaeological remains were fascinating enough, and we discovered beautifully carved and polished tools and jewellery made from conch shell (Barbados, as a coral atoll, has no natural hard stone from which to make enduring items, and any stone that is ever found has been traded from the other volcanic islands). We learned to excavate that most personal archaeological deposits, human burials, and were taught valuable lessons in field archaeology, such as how not to judge a site by its surface appearance. Who would have thought that this intimate scene of domestic life of nine hundred years earlier existed under less than thirty centimetres of sand? But for me it was the experience of working in another country, in among the community, that was by far the best.

My next adventure also involved a hell of a lot of sand, but that is definitely where the similarities ended.

BARBADIAN (BAJAN) MACARONI PIE

Serves 4 – with salad and fried flying fish. (This is Barbados's national dish – well, unofficial national dish; cou-cou – cornflour and okra – and flying fish is the official national dish.)

250 g macaroni pasta

FOR CHEESE SAUCE

2 tbsp butter	*1 clove garlic, finely minced*
2 tbsp flour	*2 tbsp tomato ketchup*
1 cup full-cream milk	*4 cups sharp cheddar cheese, grated*
pinch salt	*1 tsp English mustard (optional)*
½ onion, finely chopped	*1 tsp hot pepper sauce (optional)*
½ cup water	*pinch paprika*
pinch black pepper	*breadcrumbs*

METHOD

Cook the pasta until al dente.

In a saucepan, melt the butter then add the flour to form a paste. Slowly add warmed milk, mixing continuously to avoid lumps. Bring to the boil and reduce heat. Add salt and onion and water to loosen mix. Add pepper, garlic and ketchup and stir to combine. Add cheese, leaving a little for the baked topping, and take off the heat and mix.

Add mustard or hot sauce if you wish. Mix the cheese sauce with pasta and pour into a greased oven dish. Sprinkle with cheese, paprika and breadcrumbs and bake in oven (190° C) until golden on top.

Serve with cucumber salad and fried fish.

Oh yes, and have a rum punch handy.*

* For rum punch, try this poem:
One of sour, two of sweet,
three of strong and four of weak.
A dash of bitter and a sprinkle of spice,
served well chilled with plenty of ice.

1 measure lime juice
2 measures sugar syrup
3 measures Mount Gay rum
4 measures water or fruit juice
dash of bitters
small pinch of grated nutmeg

Mix over ice.

OF SCUD MISSILES, THE LOWEST POINT ON EARTH AND LIVING HISTORY

GUS PETRAKI: *'First Alexander doesn't record the temple's location. Then God wipes it from the earth with a volcano. Now the currents change. Lara, maybe this temple's not meant to be found.'*

LARA CROFT: *'Everything lost is meant to be found. Don't worry.'*

Lara Croft Tomb Raider: The Cradle of Life, 2003

Recently, my nephew visited us in Australia on his six-month gap year trip around the world. He arrived with the usual backpack full of dirty laundry but also with a smart phone. Now an essential part of travel, the smart phone provides a link to home, parents, friends and travel information. In this screen age we expect to be able to talk, video call and text no matter where we are.

So it seems amazing to look back only twenty-five years or so and realise that when I was sitting around a camp fire on a project in the Wadi Fidan, Jordan, I had the same ability to communicate with the outside world as the prehistoric guys whose houses we were digging up; that is, none.

The first inkling we had that something was wrong with the world was an alarming increase in military activity on the Israeli side of the desert border, less than a kilometre to our west. The dig was located in a restricted border zone in the remote southern half of the arid Jordan Valley. I remember one night watching, with a slightly sick feeling, scores of bright orange flares drift across the horizon, occasionally illuminating fleeting silhouettes of helicopter gunships that were buzzing the border, spitting snaking lines of machine-gun tracer fire into the night. This wasn't like the regular border patrol that we had seen before, but frustratingly, we had no way of discovering what was going on. There were no mobile phones and no radio reception, and no post was ever delivered to the little Bedouin camp where we were living. But news of the outside world did arrive on a regular basis in the form of a toothless and slightly deranged truck driver who delivered fresh water once every two weeks. The crystal clear and cool liquid that formed a deep, and maddeningly inviting, oasis pool at the heart of the settlement was contaminated with the lovely little parasite that causes schistosomiasis. Also known as bilharzia, this is a debilitating, and if untreated fatal, disease caused by a water-borne worm. It's estimated that 210 million people are affected by schistosomiasis, with up to 200,000 dying of the disease each year. So it was not only off limits for drinking, it was even more unpleasant to splash around in than a communal hot tub.

While the tanker replenished the water supply, the driver would hold court with the Bedouin elders. So after three days of puzzling over the antics at the border, the water truck news bulletin informed us that the famously crazy Saddam Hussein, despotic leader of Iraq, had invaded Kuwait. Not satisfied with that, he had decided it was all Israel's fault and started firing rockets at it.

We were stunned. Not at the invasion, although that was surprising, but at the fact that rockets the size of VW Kombi buses were flying overhead, carrying heavens knows what, and landing in the midst of a bunch of already cheesed-off Israelis who didn't need much provocation to give someone a good slap.

The truck driver continued his news broadcast with lots of looking around and shaking his head, and the old Bedouin guys, who were serious most of the time, became very grave and tutted. We more than tutted when it was translated to us that Israel had threatened to retaliate not only with airstrikes but with a ground invasion. There was a serious concern in the Jordanian capital, Amman, that Israeli tanks and troops were going to stomp across Jordan to take on Iraq on its western flank. As luck would have it, one of the easiest and most likely routes out of the Jordan Valley and up onto the Jordanian plateau was through our camp and up the Wadi Fidan valley. We were going to be a rather squishy speed bump in a rapidly deteriorating Middle East crisis.

This Israeli invasion – well, more like a trespass, as they didn't at that point have any beef with the Jordanians – seemed increasingly likely as Saddam's Scud missiles continued to rain down. Understandably, the Jordanian army were getting very jumpy.

Midway into this drama the project team, made up of archaeologists from all over the world, took a well-needed break to Aqaba, Jordan's tiny bit of coast to the south. We were late returning and it was dark as we travelled the valley highway through the restricted security zone along the Israeli border. The road was deserted and then, just at the midway point between nowhere and bugger all, the bus broke down.

We had been stuck on the side of the road for about an hour, chatting and watching the Israeli helicopter gunships cruise past, dropping flares and checking us out. It soon became clear that they weren't the only army interested in a stationary vehicle in the demilitarised zone, at night, in the midst of a regional security crisis. Points of light appeared on the highway and resolved into three Jordanian army vehicles. The young soldiers asked us to stay on the bus. They looked very serious and held their machine guns tightly. To begin with, we thought the whole thing a bit of a lark and started winding up the sole American team member, Earl, telling him that it didn't look good for him. But something about the attitude of the soldiers and their sergeant made us go quiet.

The night stretched on. The Israeli helicopters continued to buzz us, further aggravating the Jordanian soldiers. Another vehicle turned up and an officer stepped onto the bus, looked at us briefly and then said something to the sergeant and disappeared.

The sergeant, a silver-haired, tough-looking soldier turned to us and scowled. 'Up! Get up. You must now get off the bus.'

There was a stunned silence as we looked at each other. At these times you can rationalise all you want. You can say that Jordan is a civilised country, we're clearly not combatants or spies, everything will be fine. But when you've just been ordered off a bus at night in the middle of nowhere by gun-toting soldiers, you can't help but think you may be killed. We were ushered a little way from the bus, off the road and into the desert, where we stood in a quiet group surrounded by half a dozen soldiers. I remember the moon was up and the desert was a silver grey. It was quite beautiful and would have been a peaceful image if it hadn't been for the bright beams of the Israeli helicopter search lights.

The officer approached and said quietly in broken English. 'Knees. Now, down, please.'

There followed perhaps ten seconds when I was certain that I was going to die. Strangely, I was relieved that I was going to be shot. At least it would be quick. I remember those seconds very clearly. The dusty smell of the desert, the clatter of the helicopter blades, the faces of the team mates who I had known for only a few weeks and, of course, my heart that felt like it had grown to fill my whole chest and was trying to beat its way through my ribs.

Slowly we dropped to our knees. I think a few guys raised their arms but there was no sound.

Suddenly the officer who had just spoken hurried towards us, waving his hands. 'No, no, sorry. English no good! *Sit*, sit, rest legs, knees. Sorry, we mend engine.'

Bloody hell. Welcome to the Middle East.

*

Three weeks earlier a taxi had dropped me in the centre of Amman, and I remember Arabia hitting me around the head. I turned full circle on the spot with my pack on my back as I surveyed the planet I had landed on. It may as well have been a different planet for all the resemblance it had to anything I had experienced before. It was so hot, sweat immediately ran down my face, stinging my eyes, and my shirt stuck to my sides. There didn't seem to be any air as the buildings in this part of Amman pressed in and jumbled together, teetering over the narrow streets and scrambling over steep hills that rose all around. Dirty, weeping air-conditioning units, noisily pumping out hot air, studded the outside of apartment and office blocks that were also plastered with colourful signs advertising who knew what in curling Arabic script. Occasionally, an incongruous advert for a western and familiar product stood out. I remember Carnation Condensed Milk, Nescafé and HP Sauce seemed popular.

As I ambled along the busy streets, the crowds parted in front of me with quizzical looks and mumbled comments. I must have looked quite odd, pale, sweaty and wide-eyed, trying to take it all in. Constantly blaring horns from the gridlocked traffic tormented my ears, and the fetid bins and delicious smoky smells of street-side barbecues alternately assaulted and seduced my nose. By chance I spotted my hotel, the Bader. It was located at the end of a short, narrow alley, which was lined with restaurants and coffee shops. I got a room for a couple of nights and with great relief let my pack fall onto the bed. The room was stiflingly hot and heavy with the stench of the toilet, so I wrenched open the windows whose panes, for some inexplicable reason, were blocked out with dark blue and red paint.

I remember sitting at that open window for hours, letting the city wash over me, and I can clearly see that view now. It wasn't beautiful, in fact it was pretty ugly, but it was fascinating and took in nearly two thousand years of human history. Standing out against the drab and filthy exteriors of the modern buildings, Roman ruins of an ancient citadel crowned the hill opposite.

I could see, cut into the base of the slope below me, the columns and terraced seating of an amphitheatre which marked the centre of the hugely important ancient city of Philadelphia, a major centre of the Judean kingdom of Herod and later one of the main administrative centres of the Roman Decapolis.

Jordan, or to give its official title, the Hashemite Kingdom of Jordan, is one of the great survivors. Occupying a near landlocked position on the eastern bank of the Jordan River its borders, over Ottoman and the British occupations, changed so often they may as well have been drawn in pencil. But through all of its tumultuous history it has kept its head down and plodded on to the present day when, against all the odds, it is now a vibrant, modern country. Sure it still has many problems, particularly poverty, partly stemming from the unfortunate luck that, while surrounded by countries with some of the biggest and richest oil and gas reserves on the planet, Jordan has not a drop.

The modern country is bordered by the Jordan River, Palestine and Israel to the west, Saudi Arabia to the south and east, Iraq to the north-east and Syria to the north. As I mentioned, there's a very small coastline at the south on the Gulf of Aqaba that lies at the northern end of the Red Sea.

Aqaba is one of the few places in the world where you can observe four countries in one blink. I remember sitting on a rickety metal chair, calf-deep in the warm Red Sea waters of the Gulf of Aqaba, puffing on a *nargila* (water pipe), watching the sun set over the pink and dusty mountains of the Sinai Peninsula of Egypt. Almost at their base I could see the brightly flashing lights of the bars and discos of the party town of Eilat at the southernmost tip of Israel. Occasionally, the deep bass thump of the discos added a rude accompaniment to the haunting call to prayer and reminded me of the constant and mind-boggling incompatibilities and incongruences of this mad part of the world. To my left, and catching the last rays of the day on its naked and sunburnt hills, Saudi Arabia stretched out south into the gathering evening.

It was an extraordinary sight, and constantly during my travels through the Middle East I would have to stop and realise what I was seeing and remember where I was. It seemed that every vista and place name had jumped out of an ancient text. The past lies so thick across this land that it felt like I was wading through glue.

I've always enjoyed swearing. I'm not particularly proud of it nor do I think that I should be a role model to younger readers. But I really like swearing a lot and stringing swearwords together. I have found this to be extremely useful when confronted by extraordinary images and experiences when travelling. So I am sure (although I cannot remember) that, in between puffs on the water pipe and as I surveyed this incredible scene, I was swearing like a trooper with the wonder of it all.

You see, all this was a complete surprise to me. This was a time before TripAdvisor and online travel sites. It was the time of guidebooks and I dislike reading guidebooks. No, that's not quite correct, I don't dislike reading guidebooks. I just don't like reading them to the detriment of actually experiencing the thrill of new and unanticipated discoveries. If you read in advance everything about the Parthenon, are you going to have the same OMFG experience than if you just stumble on it as you wander around Athens? I don't want to experience the world through the jaded eye of the guidebook author, nor do I feel the need to tick off a country's highlights as if they were a shopping list. I feel it's almost equivalent to going to a great rock concert and watching the whole thing through the crappy little screen of your smart phone. I don't get that. Does anyone get that?

There was one occasion during an expedition to Syria that reinforced my pet issue with guidebooks. I'd been wandering around the fabulous city of Aleppo in northern Syria looking for the post office to check for mail (remember the days when the only contact with the outside world while travelling was receiving thin blue airmail letters, gummed down on three sides, forwarded to Poste Restante addresses?). I was standing in the shade of a great old gnarled olive tree that stood in the middle of a square teeming with people and traffic, when in the midst of the dust and blue exhaust came a woman bobbing through the crowd like a ship in full sail.

She must have been six foot in her stockinged feet and had the frame and gait of a gladiator. But it was her attire that stopped me. On her head, perched at a jaunty angle, was a wide-brimmed yellow fedora, encircled by bright silk gerberas. Her face was mostly obscured by enormous sunglasses that looked like a bat was clinging to her large nose, petrified at the thought of slipping and being munched up by her amazingly large mouth, which was in constant motion, although the general cacophony of the bus station prevented my hearing her at first.

As she ducked deftly past a water seller and the ubiquitous chewing gum hawker, the rest of her was revealed in the brilliant yellow light of the Aleppo morning. She wore a bib-fronted linen dress, which had a drop waist and reminded me of a style from a bygone era, 1920s or perhaps prewar – an impression reinforced by the numerous glass necklaces that glittered and swung madly to her waist. Thick brown tights and T-strap shoes, a handbag the size of a carpet bag and a cane-handled umbrella completed this extraordinary ensemble.

I realised with some anxiousness that she was marching across the square towards me, and then her bat wings clocked me and she raised her brolly and pointed at my chest, without breaking stride. I looked around to see if she'd been gesturing at someone else, perhaps another Edwardian flying-mammal fetishist, but no, I was alone in this part of the square.

It was at that moment I realised that *she* wasn't alone. Behind her straggled ten, no, twelve people. They looked bewildered, tired and something else. I couldn't put my finger on it straight away. Then it came to me: they reminded me of grainy black-and-white images of captured soldiers walking in a line with their hands on their heads, all with the same uncomfortable expression – defeat. This did not temper my alarm, but too late I made an effort to move off with a quickly assembled frown and purposeful step towards the Citadel.

'Hello, you!' she said.

Who says 'Hello, you'? I thought. She had the plummiest English accent and that aristocratic way of saying something as archaic as 'Hello, you' without an atom of embarrassment.

'Hi,' I said.

'Are you English?' She stopped a metre in front of me and pulled her sunglasses down to the tip of her nose so that I could see her eyes. I was surprised to see that they were twinkly, and she immediately seemed much less intimidating. Her retinue shuffled to a stop, one person almost comically bumping into the one in front. Their cameras told me they were a tour group and the woman interrogating me was their guide.

I turned to her once more and said, 'Yes,' and as that seemed insufficient, I added, 'from London. I'm working here.'

'Good for you,' she replied. 'What is it that you do, here in Syria?'

I noticed that she had moved to my side and had raised her voice so that the tour group could hear her. I had become a part of the tour.

'I'm an archaeologist. I'm heading east tomorrow to work on a dig near the Euphrates.' I smiled at the group. A few managed a fleeting grimace in return, and a couple had a *help me* look around their eyes.

'Good for you,' she said again. 'Used to dig a bit myself before my hip went. So what are you hunting? Hmm? Roman? Assyrian?'

Her dialogue was from another era. I half-expected Hercule Poirot to come shuffling round the corner.

'Bronze Age,' I replied. 'Early Bronze Age, I think. I don't know much about the site.'

'Fascinating,' she said to the assembled tour. 'The Early Bronze age is equivalent to the Protodynastic and Old Kingdom periods of Egypt and Sumeria, and Akkadian phases of Mesopotamia, and sees the development of complex settlements, writing, cuneiform in this region.'

I blinked. I guess she knew her prehistory. I say I guess because I hadn't a clue whether she was wrong or right. I hadn't been the most attentive student and anything I had learned at university seemed to have dribbled away since graduating.

As she prepared to leave, she spotted the shiny new guide to Syria in my hand and tutted.

'That thing,' she gestured at the book, 'is why there is no romance or adventure in travel anymore.' She surveyed her party and whispered to me. 'Look at them, they've been on some God-awful tour through Turkey where everything was planned, everything was known, no surprises. Picked them up an hour ago. I'll sort them out with this,' she pointed to her head, 'and this,' and she waggled a much worn copy of Baedeker's guide to Palestine and Syria. 'Dates to 1876, wonderful descriptions and all the things worth looking at were there then. I recommend the Citadel first, and don't forget to say hello to St George.'

She raised her arm like a general commanding troops to advance. 'Forward, chaps, history waits!'

'Cheerio and good luck,' she said to me and strode off across the square with the little retinue following. Lucky buggers, I thought. I looked down at my guidebook and put it away in my pack. I haven't used one since. Exploring the past is to journey into the unknown. I guess even when I'm being a tourist, I still prefer to discover the world myself instead of relying on other people's adventures.

*

Anyway, while my backpack was weighed down with the *Lonely Planet Guide to Jordan*, true to form I had only flicked through it briefly before boarding the plane at Heathrow one rainy grey June morning bound for Queen Alia Airport, five and half hours to the east.

I knew I needed to get a cab from the airport to Amman, and I had the name of two hotels downtown that I thought I would try. I also had a handful of Jordanian dinars in my pocket that I'd picked up from the small Lloyds Bank branch in the Pembrokeshire market town of Haverfordwest. It's strange to look back and realise that cheap travel, beyond package holidays to Europe, was non-existent at that time, and I remember a few oohs and aahs going on behind the counter when the strange notes were laid out. Of course, the reaction of the bank tellers was only partly because of the unusual destination but also because Jordan was often mentioned on the TV news in the same breath as Israel, Palestine and the Intifada.

Meaning 'to shake off', the Intifada was a popular uprising of Palestinians opposed to the Israeli occupation of the Palestinian territories. When I arrived in Jordan in 1990, images of stone-throwing youths in running battles with the Israeli Defence Forces had graced the TV news screens of the west for the previous three years. The conflict had caused considerable strife to the already beleaguered people on both sides, but particularly to the Palestinians in the occupied territories of the West Bank, East Jerusalem and the Gaza Strip. Jordan was often mentioned within the bulletins because of its close proximity but also because almost two million Palestinian refugees lived in Jordan, many in long-term UN refugee camps on the outskirts of Amman.

To the tellers at the bank in rural Pembrokeshire, not only was the currency alien, so was the idea of travelling to that part of the world. When I explained that I was an archaeologist and was going to dig up some old sites, everything was suddenly all right. This is a strange but quite common reaction. Archaeologists are expected to be eccentric (read: foolhardy) and to travel to exotic and dangerous places. It's what we do and I'm pretty sure this expectation goes a long way to explaining my reasons for becoming an archaeologist.

Queen Alia Airport is named after one of the late King Hussein's wives and is one of those cases where the name seems in rather bad taste or at least ironic. An example close to home is the Harold Holt Memorial Swimming Baths in Melbourne, named after the postwar prime minister who drowned while in office. Maybe this is an example of very dry Australian humour, but I doubt there was any irony when Jordan's main airport was named after a former queen who died in an air crash.

The airport lies twenty kilometres to the south of Amman and the taxi rattled along the dark-grey highway that cut through the desert. It whizzed past huddles of concrete compounds where trees and strangely unfinished-looking flat-roofed houses peeked above the rough blockwork walls. Only completed houses were liable for rates charges, so consequently every house had rusty red reinforcing bars and unfinished concrete columns standing on the roofs of clearly occupied dwellings.

Little lads in dusty dishdashas (long robes) and young girls in jelly sandals and headscarves lazily stumbled behind flocks of goats. They held long sticks above their heads, like tour guides with their *Follow me* flags, and occasionally brought them down with a flick onto the behinds of any of their charges that dawdled too long at a thorny shrub.

It was summer, a crazy time to contemplate a dig, and the sun was fierce and bounced up off the pale dirt and rock and the whitewashed buildings. The pungent smell of slow-burning rubbish, a sickly heavy odour, cut through the heavy fug of cigarette smoke that swirled around inside the cab. Smoke rose languidly from half-rotting, half-smouldering piles of garbage that sprawled next to the highway. Then I realised what the tiny flashes of colour were that twinkled off every bush and shrub as far as I could see. Sarcastically called the Jordan desert rose, they were tattered plastic bags that had escaped these garbage piles only to be caught on the branches of the sparse plants that dotted the desert.

The taxi driver looked about forty and wore a red-checked keffiyeh (traditional headdress) and white dishdasha. A lustrous black moustache completed the unofficial uniform of the Jordanian male. Smoking constantly, he clicked through a bright green loop of prayer beads and nodded along to music that rose above the whistle of air rushing through the open windows.

Occasionally, he flicked channels on the radio and found another distinctly Arabic-sounding tune with lots of staccato violins and a male voice almost ululating, probably about forbidden love (they almost always were). The driver looked in the rear-view mirror at me. 'Good?' he said and flicked his right hand, palm up, in that international gesture of, *Well, what do you think?* I nodded and not for the last time wished I had learned Arabic, even the basics, before I'd embarked on this trip.

I spent almost two years living and working in Jordan in the early 1990s and those times have left a lasting impression on me. They were a formative period for me, contributing significantly to who I am and how I regard archaeology and the past.

All the sites that I worked on in Jordan dated to prehistoric periods. As I have mentioned, archaeology is a broad subject and incorporates dozens of specialty fields. Some of these fields are based on subject matter and some are defined by periods in time. The human past can be broadly divided into two time periods: prehistory and history. At its simplest (though, like any other part of archaeology and history, there is no such thing), prehistory refers to all of the past prior to the appearance of the written record, after which the past is referred to as history. While there are endless arguments about when this dividing line falls, or indeed whether it is a valid definition, I think it is useful to consider the human story as just that – a story that hasn't yet finished, so prehistory to history is a transition from one chapter to another. Mind you, it's an incredibly significant transition and arguably the biggest and most important change since our ancestors decided to stand on two legs and do a bit of DIY.

Essentially, the transition between prehistory and history started thousands of years before the invention of writing, when people moved from hunter-gathering to farming. This fundamental change fascinated me when I was at university and still does.

Hunter-gathering refers to a way of life where the calories required by an individual, or at most an extended family unit, are gained through gathering fruit, seeds, nuts and other plant material from locations where they naturally grow, supplemented with animal protein and fat from the fishing and hunting of wild animals. Hunter-gatherers, particularly in sub-tropical and temperate climates, also have a propensity to be nomadic, following seasonal availability of plant food and animals. There are very few communities that practise this way of life anymore; the Hadza are a people that continue this prehistoric way of life where it was invented, in the east African Rift Valley. But for over 200,000 years, this model of subsistence with subtle regional variances was the only way of life. Foraging for food and occasionally spearing a fish or knocking something over the head took on average an hour or two a day to satisfy the needs of the group. The rest of the day was filled with hanging around, devising complicated origin stories, and rules and regulations about who should marry who to avoid the grandkids being born with too many fingers.

About twenty thousand years ago, this lifestyle, which on the surface has a lot going for it, began to change. Archaeological discoveries show that, starting in what is known as the Levant (the eastern Mediterranean, including Lebanon, Syria, Jordan, Palestine, Israel), people stopped roaming the landscape and started to settle down and build houses. Prior to this period, it is assumed that shelter was rudimentary or movable, such as caves or tents. In addition to putting down roots in the mud-bricks and mortar sense, they also literally put down roots by deliberately collecting food plant seeds and planting them near to where they lived.

These farmers got into GM cropping by carefully selecting the genetic mutants of their favourite food plants with characteristics that made their lives easier. Examples are the early forms of wheat and barley called emmer wheat and einkorn barley. Both are indigenous to the Levant and these grains are the prime candidates for why the whole subsistence revolution took off in this part of the world. For a long time the wild types had been gathered from, well, the wild. Then wild types were planted near the new settlements, but the harvesting was still pretty tricky because the plant naturally wants to propagate itself by dropping its seed when the time is right. For our early farmers that meant either taking the grain heads when they were not ripe, before they have fallen to the ground, or spending a hell of a lot of the late summer on their hands and knees, picking the grains from the surface of the fields. Occasionally, individual plants among the wild stock would have a mutation that meant the grains remained on the stalk even when they were ripe. The little stem that attached the grain to the stalk, which normally shrivelled up and broke when the time was right, failed to do so in these individuals. In normal circumstances this genetic aberration never got any further as its grain, containing the genetic information, died on the stalk and never reached the ground. But to the early farmers, they were the answer to mouldy grain and bad backs. So these mutants were selected and grown, and the grain was harvested and planted until they had fields of wheat and barley that ripened on the stalk and could be harvested directly from the plant.

Then they turned their attention to animals. Previously, most species of animals in the region were killed and eaten, worn or both. But our early farmers were too busy building houses and tending their fields to go trotting around the landscape after animals, some of which were just as likely to turn around and start trotting after them. So they selected the least dangerous and plumpest animals and set to domesticating them so that they would tolerate being pushed around by kids with sticks. This perhaps explains why bears and wolves dropped off the menu.

Simple enough. Except of course that it isn't. Not only are the processes of domestication of plants and animals difficult and slow, the whole way of life of these early farmers in Jordan and elsewhere became increasingly complex. As a hunter-gatherer, life was pretty simple. It was their own choice if they wanted to make it complicated with traditions and taboos.

But as a farmer starting out ten thousand years ago, you had to learn to build, make new tools for new jobs, plant crops, irrigate the land, harvest and process the grain, harness fire in new things called ovens, learn new recipes, store and account for surplus harvest; the list goes on. The quest to find out why these communities so long ago decided to do all this was why I was in Jordan. And I wasn't alone. Expeditions from universities all over the world were scratching around sites throughout the Middle East.

The site in the Wadi Fidan dated to this transitional period and was one of the most interesting sites that I worked on in Jordan. *Wadi* is an Arabic term for a river valley, invariably a dry one. It was my first project in the Middle East and was also without doubt the most challenging, so it's perhaps a reflection on my sanity that I came back and worked on half a dozen more.

After a couple of days finding my feet in Amman, I met up with the rest of the expedition team at the then gleamingly new American Center for Oriental Research (ACOR) in the Tla Al Ali district in the north-west of the city. The director was a short, stout man who was softly spoken and had a gentle but determined look. The team included a bunch of students from the Institute of Archaeology in London and Sheffield University, a couple from Switzerland, a few from Holland and Germany and an American guy called Earl. There were about fifteen of us all up and everyone seemed eager to get started.

The first sign that things were going to be 'interesting' was the additional official paperwork we all needed to get to the site. The Wadi Fidan curls down from the craggy desert plateau that makes up the central part of Jordan into the great Rift Valley through which the River Jordan flows and the Dead Sea evaporates. Our destination was a little island in the middle of a parched alluvial fan at the bottom of the Jordan Valley, to the south of the Dead Sea. Not only were we going to be digging during the Middle-Eastern summer but we were going to be digging at the lowest point on earth at the hottest time of the year. The extra paperwork was not so that our bleached and desiccated corpses could be identified and sent to our families. No, it was because the site was less than a thousand metres from the Jordan–Israel border, one of the most fought-over stretches of Godforsaken desert, rock and salt pan anywhere in the world, and we needed special security clearance (oh joy), presumably so that our *bullet-riddled*, bleached and desiccated corpses could be identified and sent to our families.

Two days later we found ourselves huddled under an old army tarpaulin, eyes screwed up against the heat shimmer, watching the Israeli border patrols menace the near distance. Frequent flashes of light told us that they were watching us too and probably wondering who the hell we were and what we were doing. By the middle of the day most of us couldn't answer the first and were definitely questioning the second.

The living conditions were remote, bleak, unsanitary and dangerous. In the 1980s, in a classically misguided gesture, the South Koreans decided to build a load of schools for established Bedouin communities in the rural parts of Jordan. Maybe someone raised the question of powering these schools, maintaining them or even staffing them, but if they did, they were not taken very seriously, so dozens of concrete block schools litter the landscape. Most have never been used unless you count occasional stops by a passing goatherd caught short.

The derelict concrete school that we called home for nearly four months lay at the end of a twenty-kilometre dirt road that led off the Jordan Valley highway an hour to the south of the Dead Sea. While it was remote, we weren't lonely, as a small Bedouin community lived near to the school around an oasis spring.

Apart from the vibrant and luscious green vegetation that surrounded the spring, the rest of the landscape was bleak. The shattered and scree-scarred cliffs of the Jordanian side of the Rift Valley rose a thousand metres to our east, and its crumbling lower slopes were all we could see to the north and south. West lay the valley bottom, barren and cut with shallow flood channels and studded with dull lifeless shrubs that disappeared in the liquid heat haze. Above the mirages and the dust devils (mini tornadoes) that stalked the valley bottom, you could see the dark blue hills of the Negev, the biblical wilderness where Christ spent forty days and forty nights confronting the Devil. I knew how he felt.

The accommodation was basic, army cots for beds, a couple of trestle tables and two chairs for artefact work and a two-burner gas stove. Washing was with a bucket of water and a cup in a shielded corner behind the teacher's house. The old school toilet block had never been plumbed in and was blocked, but that's all we had.

It was up to each team member to look after their own welfare and safety; the most basic amenities for such a remote location, for example, soap, a first-aid kit, a fridge, chairs, were apparently optional. A roster was set up to cook and clean for the team, as there were insufficient funds to hire a project cook. When you started work at 4am, the last thing you wanted to do was bookend the day by cooking for fifteen and cleaning the bogs. But archaeologists are doughty souls and we put up with the privations.

Well, most of us did. One day about two weeks into the project, and during a particularly fierce hot spell, we wearily got out of the Land Rover after a day on site to find the camp in turmoil. The director was standing in the yard looking shaken and staring into the teacher's house, which was used as the project lab and work rooms. There were buckets and paper strewn at the front door and crashing sounds coming from inside. Before we could ask what was going on, there was a squeal and one of the Swiss girls came running out of the building, shouting something and bolting behind us. A mad roar was followed by an alarming crunching coming from the far-side opening (none of the buildings had windows or doors).

No one said anything, but we all looked at the director. We guessed what had happened; it had been brewing for days and we had warned him to do something. One of the guys was a tall, lumbering and initially quite amiable fellow, who on arrival at the school had almost broken down and then stomped off to a nearby hill and sat there until dark. We had sympathised with him at first; after all, it was pretty rough accommodation. But it all got weirder when he declared that he couldn't go out on site as it was too hot, and when we came back each day dusty and parched, he greeted us with a blank look. At night around the camp fire he rambled on with the other expedition weirdo, a guy who only walked on his tiptoes (you couldn't make this up), talked about slasher movies, and cracked jokes about pretty much any offensive and downright screwed-up subject he could think of.

The rest of us got really concerned. This guy was not the kind of person you wanted going all Jack Nicholson on you when the nearest police station was a four-hour drive away. Worse still, he was getting increasingly aggressive and so was our twinkle-toes. In answer to our concerns, the director told us to relax and that he would probably settle down when he got used to the heat.

As he now went about destroying the project office, one of the more sardonic Dutch guys said to the director, 'He seems to be getting the hang of the heat, then.'

We all sat in the shade on the other side of the compound and watched as the director tried to talk him down. As bits of broken chair and table flew through the gaps in the walls, it seemed that he wasn't quite ready to engage. Eventually, he was found curled in a ball, holding his head and whispering, 'The heat, the heat.' He left in a taxi that day, still with his eyes cast to the ground, and we all breathed a sigh of relief. A year later I saw him again in London at a Society of Antiquities talk. He greeted me as an old friend and chatted away as if nothing had happened, although he did say that he'd shifted his area of interest to Scandinavia.

There were three archaeological sites strung out along the Wadi Fidan that we were investigating. One was a chalcolithic period (4300–3300 BC – or 6300–5300 years ago) site, which had very early evidence of copper smelting, the first metal that was systematically manufactured, followed by bronze and then iron.

The three-age system defines in broad terms the major developments in human history based on their advances in technological achievement. The three main ages, Stone, Bronze and Iron, were first devised in the early nineteenth century by the Danish archaeologist Christian Jürgensen Thomsen. The Stone, or Palaeolithic, Age includes all the aeons for which (pardon the pun) stone was the cutting edge in tools. The Bronze Age includes the advent of a huge advance in technology, with the discovery of smelting and forging objects out of metal. Firstly copper, then an alloy of copper and tin that produces bronze, a harder metal more suited to tool and weapon manufacture. The final age, the Iron Age, corresponds to not only the invention of iron but the beginning of the classical era. The system may be two hundred years old but it's still broadly used.

The other two sites were what are described as Pre-Pottery Neolithic sites and dated to around ten thousand years ago. As the name suggests, they showed evidence of a Neolithic culture, that is, the development of smaller and more technically advanced stone tools (the new (*neo*) stone (*lithic*) age) used to perform new tasks such as scything crops and the construction of permanent dwellings. But the lack of pottery suggested that they dated to the earlier phase of the transition from hunter-gatherers to farmers. The site I worked on stood at the peak of a small mound surrounded on all sides by the alluvial fan of the wadi, which spread out across the floor of the Jordan Valley. The archaeological deposits that we uncovered were well preserved and rare. Various specialists came to see the site during the course of the dig to nod and exclaim rather bitterly that it was amazing. Bitterly, because by now we had realised that the director was disliked by most archaeologists working in Jordan, and they couldn't stand it that he'd found such a site.

My site was an uncomfortable, bumpy hour's drive from camp so, mercifully, we were spared most of the director's visits. We spent many an hour going delirious uncovering the remarkably preserved walls and floors of buildings that had dropped out of sight and mind six hundred generations ago, six thousand years before the construction of the Great Pyramid at Giza.

Perched on a mound in the middle of nowhere, we discovered stone walls standing head-high, still with patches of plaster painted with red pigment. A small dome-shaped oven was discovered built into one of the walls and I believe it is still thought to be the oldest oven in Jordan, if not the whole of the Middle East. The artefacts were finely made stone tools, sickle blades and points, which suggested that the landscape was a lot wetter and lusher back then, able to sustain fields and animals large enough to throw things at. But why these people decided to settle down and do a kitchen makeover remained elusive. There is only so much that chipped stones and tumbled walls can tell about our past; many of their motives and practices have left no trace.

Unfortunately, our enthusiasm for these ancient ruins was tempered by our incident on the dark highway and the increasing tensions caused by Saddam Hussein's antics. The final few weeks of the project were tense. Tempers, already strained by the poor living conditions, flared, and it was with huge relief and not a backward glance that we all headed back to Amman.

The capital was in an almost carnival mood. The various wars since Israel's declaration of independence in 1948 had resulted in both the loss of the West Bank, previously the most productive part of Jordan, and the influx of millions of Palestinian refugees. Many of these refugees had been living in UN camps on the edges of Amman since the 1948 war, graduating slowly from army tents to tiny concrete block units, crammed together with only the most basic amenities. So when I was confronted by t-shirts, caps and watches emblazoned with Saddam Hussein's face and crudely carved wooden Scud missiles painted in the Iraqi colours being sold on every street corner in Amman, I was not surprised.

Jordan had walked a difficult path in forging neutral, if not entirely peaceful, relations with Israel without incurring the wrath of the more militant members of the Arab League and the Palestinian peoples living in Jordan. King Hussein and his government were certainly not foolish enough to stop the groundswell of support for the strongarm tactics of Saddam against their old foe. Mercifully for the Jordanians, the missile attacks stopped and Israel resisted Saddam's provocations, but it was a close-run thing.

I was tired and decided to take some rest and recuperation before heading to my next dig. As if I hadn't had enough insanity, I decided to head over the border into Israel and stay in Jerusalem.

*

Jerusalem is the most incredible city in the world. It is also the nuttiest place I have ever been. It's like a medieval Las Vegas but without the poker tables and with a lot more craziness. Even writing its name makes me almost gasp, and I've only been there once, for a week.

At the time it was quite difficult to cross the border between Jordan and Israel. It could be done, but if you got an Israeli stamp in your passport it was likely that you wouldn't get back into Jordan and less likely that you would be issued with a work permit, so that risk put a lot of archaeologists off. I suspect that actually it wasn't that great, and as it turned out, the Israelis were quite happy to stamp a piece of paper rather than your passport at the border controls.

I remember the journey from the Allenby (or King Hussein) Bridge that crosses the River Jordan and forms the only access to the West Bank. From the window of a crowded minibus, I looked at the rocky and desolate landscape as we climbed out of the valley and struck west. It looked the same as the Jordanian side, apart from the distinctive blue and white flags depicting the Star of David, the Israeli national flag, which fluttered from public buildings. But it was different, it felt different. It was the Holy Land – never mind that Jordan was also part of the ancient lands described in the Old Testament, it was this western side of the Jordan River that was the focus of the holy texts and the events surrounding the life of Jesus Christ.

I was brought up in a non-religious household. Mum was born in Dublin and brought up in the Catholic faith, my father in a Methodist home, but neither was religious. However, both believed that it was important to get some knowledge at school, reasoning that religion was the framework of most of modern society's inner workings: laws, the judiciary, the working week, national holidays. Here in Israel, and especially in the city that loomed before me on the Judean tablelands, knowing something about religion made a great deal of sense.

Jerusalem is one of the most significant places for the devoted followers of the three main Abrahamic religions – Islam, Judaism and Christianity – and I was completely unprepared for what that really meant on the ground. Jerusalem is a place where archaeology exists in the past and the present and so, to an archaeologist, it is fascinating. Prehistoric sites rub shoulders with Old Testament ruins, and Roman monuments decorate the medieval city. But they are not only relics of a past city. They are integral to the lives of modern Jerusalemites.

The bus dropped me off in the chaotic square outside Damascus Gate at the north of the Old City. Like most cities that have their origins in antiquity and have muddled through to the present day, Jerusalem has an old centre ringed by modern, or at least more recent, suburbs. The bus station outside Damascus Gate was the typical scruffy concrete, no-nonsense utilitarian architecture that is seen across the Middle East region. But as I passed under the hulking medieval arch that pierced the high wall surrounding the ancient square mile of the Old City, the modern world disappeared, replaced by another reality, which seemed to be about half past ten in the morning somewhere in the fifteenth century. Like Lucy glimpsing Narnia for the first time over the snow-dusted shoulder of a fur coat in the great wardrobe, or Dorothy during her technicolour vision of Oz, I stumbled to a halt and stared.

Crumbling buildings misshapen by hundreds of years of ill-considered repairs and additions leered over narrow alleyways that wandered off in different directions. Tourists like me stood staring, while locals weaved around them in and out of tiny shops and along worn cobbled ways.

There are old places in the world that, while they really are old and often quite beautiful, have become 'Ye Olde Worlde', twee and fake, like the Disneyland Castle (the French Quarter in New Orleans, Dingle in County Kerry, The Rocks in Sydney spring to mind). Not so here. Despite the tourists, the odd souvenir seller and the hype, the Old City of Jerusalem is the real deal. A place where people have done their thing and where others, like me, have come to see them doing it, for thousands of years.

I spent a week living in the Arab Quarter and wandered the narrow laneways, lost, for most of the time. It was an extraordinary experience. Split into four distinct parts – the Arab, Jewish, Armenian and Christian quarters – the city also contains three incredibly sacred religious sites: the Church of the Holy Sepulchre (the location of Christ's crucifixion and tomb), the Temple Mount and Western Wall (the site of the first and second temples of Solomon and the Holy of Holies) and the Dome of the Rock and Al-Aqsa Mosque (the location of the ascension of Mohammed). In what can only be described as a town-planning error of biblical proportions, the last two occupy the same location. The ultimate salvation of the Jews with the arrival of the Messiah will only happen when a temple once more sits atop the Temple Mount. The foundations of the previous two temples, destroyed first by the Babylonians in 586 BC and then by the Romans (of course) in 70 AD, form the lower parts of the Western Wall, and it is in bitter remembrance of these attacks that Jews visit the wall in tears. The rock that lies at the centre of the Dome of the Rock, the Foundation Stone, is the most holy location in Judaism and they are not allowed to visit it. Honestly, you couldn't make it up.

A large population of the Old City is made up of officials and servants of the various traditions and multitude denominations. So not only do you have a potent mix of Orthodox Jews rubbing shoulders with Muslims – 'Can we build our Temple please?' 'No, sorry' – you have all the various sects that bicker among themselves. And there is no place where this is taken to more Monty Python-esque levels than at the Church of the Holy Sepulchre. Located on the supposed site of Calvary, the place of Christ's execution, there has been a church here since the Roman Emperor Constantine ordered one to be built in 325 AD.

The details of the carve-up of the holiest church in Christendom would fill a book, so I won't go into them, but in brief, the huge, rambling building is occupied and variously maintained by half a dozen or so Christian orders. Known as a simultaneum, or shared church, it is home to the Eastern Orthodox, Oriental Orthodox and Roman Catholic traditions. On a day-to-day basis, the peace is maintained by strict appliance of the Status Quo. Developed in 1853, the Status Quo aimed to halt the frequent bloody battles among the groups over things like religious service times and responsibilities for the maintenance and repair of various parts of the building. It lays out strict times of prayer and services within the common areas so that Greek Orthodox and Ethiopian Coptics don't punch on during evensong.

As I mentioned, various groups live within the church, some on the roof, and each group merrily adorns and maintains its own areas, shrines etc. Unfortunately, the Status Quo is a bit vague on who has responsibility to manage and maintain the common areas. Confusion over which group has the right or honour to occupy or carry out work in these areas frequently results in absurd escalations of violence and pettiness.

In 2002 a Greek monk made what turned out to be a near fatal error by moving his chair from an agreed spot into the shade of a tree on one of the roof terraces. The Ethiopians, enraged by such a provocative and hostile move, went in with habits flying and arms windmilling. By the time the long-suffering police had broken it up, many lay injured, eleven seriously.

Because no one knows who is responsible for the care of large parts of the building, the church is in a perilous state of disrepair. Significant elements of the structure are unstable, and broken antique hand-blown light bulbs coated in decades of dust hang from frayed wiring because no one knows who has the honour of changing them.

The most famous example of the whole silly situation is the Immovable Ladder, a small timber ladder that rests against the front of the church above the main entrance. If you look on Google Street View, you will see it on the pediment above the door, somehow managing to look a bit self-conscious. Made of cedar, it was first mentioned in 1757 and has remained in that spot since then. In 1967 Pope Paul VI decreed that it was not to be moved (honestly, this is true, a Papal Decree ...) until the Catholic Church and the Orthodox Church are once again unified.

You can only imagine that Jesus might be thinking that perhaps they'd missed the point.

Lunacy isn't restricted to servants of the various traditions. Turning a corner one evening as I headed towards the Jaffa Gate for a happy-hour pint or two at the Arizona Bar in West Jerusalem, I bumped into a plump middle-aged woman who was walking backwards and holding a video camera to her weeping face. I'd been in Jerusalem for two days, so this hardly raised an eyebrow, but when I looked at what she was filming, both brows disappeared into my hairline. A man, also rather portly and middle-aged, was staggering towards her. He too shook with great gasping sobs and his tears mingled with lines of blood that were dribbling down his beetroot-red and sweaty face. The blood was leaking from various punctures caused by a nasty-looking crown of thorns that sat at a jaunty angle on his head. His florid and damp complexion possibly reflected the effort he was putting in to drag a very large wooden cross over the cobblestones.

This was the most involved of the pilgrims I had witnessed walking along the most famous path in Jerusalem, the Via Dolorosa (the 'Way of Grief' or 'Way of Sorrow' or 'Way of Suffering' ... you get the picture). Tradition has it that this was the route taken by Jesus to his place of execution on Skull Hill, Golgotha (to give Calvary its Aramaic name), the original processional way that is represented in all Catholic churches by the fourteen Stations of the Cross, which mark the important events that occurred on Christ's final journey. The Via Dolorosa wends its way from Lion Gate to the Church of the Holy Sepulchre and is probably the most common location for tourists to succumb to Jerusalem Syndrome. Fully acknowledged as a real syndrome, it describes the actions of tourists who go completely barking after being confronted with too much religion. I saw people who had clearly arrived as tourists but never left. They drifted around the alleys, and if they stopped to talk they would look at your ear as they spoke. Others shunned their normal clothes and wore sheets as togas. Some cases require hospitalisation (such as our man with the cross) but most recover once removed from the Holy City.

And I can completely understand where they are coming from. Not that I was tempted to re-enact the crucifixion, but I was caught up in the crazy energy of the place. On a typical walk you could expect to bump into fur-hatted Jews in full orthodox regalia heading to the synagogue, a laneway of Arab Muslims kneeling towards Mecca and black-hooded monks swinging incense and chanting a prayer. So much passion, elation, grief, distrust and implicit belief, all within the claustrophobic and time-textured spaces of the Old City.

It made the hair stand up on the back of my neck and, after a day among it all, it sent me stumbling and slightly wild-eyed out of Jaffa Gate and into the here and now (or more accurately there and then) of happy hour and the English Premier League at the Arizona Bar.

As I said. The most incredible and craziest city in the world.

OF SPYING ON SALAD, FOLLOWING AGATHA CHRISTIE AND GETTING CAUGHT SHORT

It takes very special qualities to devote one's life to problems with no attainable solutions and to poking around in dead people's garbage: words like 'masochistic', 'nosy,' and 'completely batty' spring to mind.

Paul Bahn, *The Bluffer's Guide to Archaeology*, 2007

The bus journey between Amman, capital of the Hashemite Kingdom of Jordan, and the Syrian capital may have taken only a few hours, but Damascus was a very different Arab city to the one I had just left.

I'd heard, through the archaeology rumour mills, horror stories of abductions and disappearances of foreign nationals, and that Syria was a police state. But with the bulletproof armour of youth and naivety, I'd laughed them off. I was joining an international expedition to dig a Bronze Age site on the fabled Euphrates River and I was jumping with excitement. However, a growing unease filled me as I took a short taxi trip from the bus station to downtown Damascus. Everywhere I looked there were images of the Syrian president at the time, Hafez al-Assad, staring back at me. His picture hung from every lamp post, and ten-storey-high billboards of his head adorned the sides of buildings. A little laminated photo of him, edged with gold tassels, swung wildly from the rear-view mirror of the taxi as it wove through the mad traffic.

Hafez al-Assad, father of current Syrian leader Bashar, gained power in 1970. He established a one-party revolutionary state and, closely following the *So You Want To Be a Dictator* handbook, disguised his ruthless leadership in a cult of personality. (As if wallpapering the country with your picture somehow makes the crimes against humanity all okay, because such a photogenic and obviously popular guy can't be all bad.)

While it's true the country experienced a period of increased stability and economic development, the Syrians were in fact in thrall to a paranoid leader who brutally put down any opposition. Dissent was met with immediate arrest, often followed by torture and execution. Assad set up an extraordinary network of spies and informers and enforcers to ensure the unquestioning loyalty of the people. The Mukhabarat (the Syrian secret police) were everywhere, but from my experience they had a lot to learn about secrecy, starting with its definition. But even the sunglasses-wearing spooks were not quite as obvious as the military arm of Assad's so-called ideal society.

Every other person I could see was wearing a military uniform and swinging a bloody great big gun. There were so many military types they didn't seem to know what to do with themselves. Some stood guarding pedestrian crossings, while small huddles of machine-gun-toting youths circled telephone booths. Some stood chain-smoking on traffic islands, others shuffled self-consciously next to post boxes. Whole platoons milled around every government building.

It seemed a threatening place from the rear seat of the cab, and my thoughts turned to a conversation that I'd had the previous night. It had started off as a normal chat but became weird when the woman I was talking to displayed an unusual interest in vegetables.

'Tomatoes?' I said, looking down suspiciously at my drink. 'You want me to tell you how much tomatoes are in Syria?' I looked back at the attractive diplomat, who, up to that point, I'd been trying to chat up.

She laughed. 'It's not that we are interested in tomatoes or indeed any other vegetable in particular. But we have found it's the seemingly mundane information about a place, such as the price of vegetables, that provides very useful context for, umm, other information.' The emphasis on the word *other* and a meaningful cock of an eyebrow was followed by a conspiratorial clink of our champagne glasses.

I was at a British Embassy reception in Amman, it was 1991, and I had just been asked to spy for my country.

I occasionally got invitations to these parties to provide 'interesting' conversation. I would hoover up all the finger food and drain the bar in exchange for perking up diplomatic soirees with tales of dirt and adventure.

'Are you asking me to spy for you?' I asked, forever quick on the uptake.

The diplomat frowned. '"Spy" is such a dirty word, don't you think? All we'd like you to do is note down the price and availability of basic foodstuffs in the village you'll be staying in.'

She continued, 'Also, it would be a great help if you could let us know if there are any school teachers, post offices, telephones, that kind of thing.' She looked away again and waved at someone across the other side of the reception party. Through a smile she said, 'Of course, if you see any military action or fighting, we would be very interested as well.'

I nearly choked on my drink.

'Well? What do you say?'

I wondered what fate awaited a spy captured in Syria. 'Oh, all right.' After all, it was only salad.

Besides, the chance to become an 'archaeologist spy' gave me the opportunity to join an illustrious and surprisingly large club. Over the centuries, scores of seemingly benign academics have flown under the radar of the most watchful regimes, venturing forth to remote and often dangerous corners of the world to dig the secrets of the past and nose around in the present. As far back as the fifteenth century, Cyriacus of Ancona, an Italian merchant considered by many scholars to be the father of archaeology, spied for the Vatican while he travelled around the Ottoman Empire recording hundreds of classical ruins.

At the outbreak of the Great War, TE Lawrence (aka Lawrence of Arabia) and the extraordinary character Gertrude Bell, both accomplished archaeologists and Middle Eastern experts, spied for the British. While working on the great Hittite city of Carchemish, Lawrence monitored the progress of German engineers building a railway to link Berlin to Baghdad, which aimed to dodge the British-controlled Suez Canal and secure vital oil supplies for the German war machine. Bell worked out of Cairo and Baghdad and used her amazing energy and detailed knowledge of the regions' people and landscape to aid the Allied campaign.

Later in the war, Lawrence, of course, was pivotal in supporting the Arab Revolt, which was crucial in the defeat of the Ottomans. When the combined forces of Sharif Hussein bin Ali and the British defeated Mehmed VI's army in 1918, it marked the end of one of the greatest empires in history. For over six hundred years the Ottomans had ruled a hugely diverse and vibrant empire that stretched from Algeria to Yemen and Vienna to Eritrea.

Conversely, it was the beginning of Britain's influence in the Middle East. At that time the countries of Lebanon, Syria, Israel and Jordan didn't exist, with the area collectively known as Greater Syria. At the end of the First World War, it was agreed, probably over a hearty lunch and a few brandies, that France would take the north and Britain the southern half of the region. France separated the predominately Christian lands to the west, calling them Lebanon, and labelled the remainder to the east Syria. Initially the southern partition was called Palestine, but Britain almost immediately divided the land along the River Jordan, with all the lands to the west remaining Palestine and land to the east becoming Trans-Jordan.

(Still on the subject of large lunches, it is alleged that after a particularly generous meal, Winston Churchill, then secretary of state for the British colonies, hiccuped while drawing the new border of Trans-Jordan, resulting in a huge zigzag in the eastern border with Saudi Arabia. Churchill didn't bother to rectify the slip and the border remains as it was drawn.)

The fragile friendship between the Arabs and Britain crumbled when, in response to the atrocities of the Holocaust, Britain dissolved its mandate over Palestine and supported the establishment of the Jewish state of Israel. The Arabs saw this as a huge betrayal and the rest, as they say, is history. A bloody and tragic history for all sides ever since.

The 'archaeologist spy' was not restricted to the British. The Americans had the same idea. Also during the First World War, they fielded the Mayan specialist and archaeologist Sylvanus Morley (with a name like that, could he be anything other than underhanded?) to hunt out German radio and submarine bases along the Honduras coast. He proved a daring and excellent spy and it is thought this dashing, adventurous archaeologist was an inspiration for Indiana Jones.

During the Second World War and the following decades of the Cold War, archaeologists were frequently co-opted by the CIA and SIS (the British Secret Intelligence Service, better known as MI6). In 1940 J Edgar Hoover, the great spymaster, noted that the use of archaeologists for intelligence gathering was an 'important component of a comprehensive intelligence effort'.

So it wasn't a surprise that I got asked to spy for my country. But with all this cloak and trowel stuff, it was a surprise that sites got dug at all.

Within an hour of arriving in Damascus, my decision to do my bit for Queen and Country didn't seem such a good idea after all. The taxi dropped me at a cheap hotel not far from the Citadel and the Old City. As was common practice in the Middle East, I handed over my passport to the old porter behind the tiny reception desk. I always felt uncomfortable surrendering such a valuable document, particularly as more often than not it was thrown casually into an unlocked drawer.

This time my discomfort jumped over unease and headed straight for alarm when I saw the hotel porter flick open my passport to the identification page, pick up the phone and dial a number. He didn't even have the subtlety to wait a minute until the creaky old lift arrived to whisk me to my grubby little room.

I remember thinking, *Bloody hell*, as the lift doors closed. I felt guilty and I hadn't even caught a glimpse of a tomato.

It was still early evening, so I decided to drop my kit and head out for a beer and some food. I set out for the Old City, a couple of blocks to the east, and stopped at the first corner to get my bearings and take in the sights and sounds and smells of the oldest continuously inhabited city in the world. It was dirty, it smelled and it needed everyone to stop leaning on their sodding car horns. But apart from that, it had an energy, like Jerusalem, that made the hair on the back of your neck stand up. It was just as I had hoped.

The sidewalks were clear, as most Damascenes had headed home for dinner, so I spotted the two guys straight away. They were looking in a shop window about thirty metres down the street. One wore a black leather jacket over a shirt and tie and had shiny grey 'stay press' pants. The other wore a charcoal grey double-breasted suit that was also wonderfully shiny. They both wore aviator sunglasses and Tom Selleck moustaches and seemed to be very engrossed in not looking in my direction.

'You've got to be kidding,' I said out loud. I'd been an international spy for only a day, but I reckoned I could spot a poorly disguised tail when I saw it. I strode off in search of a restaurant and within minutes it was clear that I was being followed. To begin with I was quite amused, but as I sat at a restaurant watching them order tea a few tables away, I couldn't shake the conversation at the British Embassy. Did the Syrians know or did they just mistrust all visitors? I never found out for sure, but I figured if I knew the history of archaeologists and espionage, the Syrians probably did as well.

For the next four days I was accompanied everywhere on my wanderings by two members of the secret police. I felt sorry for them as I walked for miles around the fascinating city, and sometimes they looked thoroughly cheesed off as I wove my way through the narrow streets in the hot afternoon sun. But sympathy soon gave way to annoyance as I started to feel hemmed in by a situation that was becoming farcical. I couldn't stop to look around, because when I did they would go into a right flap about looking nonchalant. Instead, they looked absurd. I recall an incident when I realised I'd gone the wrong way along the brilliantly named 'Street Called Straight' (it was quite straight). Forgetting momentarily about my followers, I turned around and started heading back the way I had come. They both stopped dead and spun away from each other. One stared into a shoe shop, the other, rigid backed, stood facing a tree trunk until I had walked silently between them.

Apart from this inconvenience and my initial fears, I never felt threatened nor was I ever approached. I suppose there's a thin and dusty file somewhere within a secret Syrian ministry with my name on it, perhaps with a stamp saying, 'Mostly walks.'

As with Jerusalem, the crumbling walls of Damascus, huge and impressive, enveloped an ancient city crowded with madrasas (Islamic schools), medieval churches, mosques, caravanserais and ruins. Weaving through everything, narrow streets burrowed beneath overhanging façades of old merchant houses, ducked under stone arches and passed ancient iron-studded gates. It was claustrophobic among the busy crowds that shuffled and jostled along these lanes, but occasionally you popped out into quiet leafy squares that lay just beyond the thoroughfares.

It was in one such square that I stopped and stared at a scene that could have fallen from the pages of *One Thousand and One Nights*. Small groups of men sat quietly in the shade of twisted old trees or under stone-arched colonnades, dressed in elaborate costumes of what I guess was the late Ottoman era. On their heads were distinctive fez headdresses of deep red wrapped round with a white turban. Under these, angular and lined faces the colour of cigars wore black moustaches and beards that flowed over white shirts. The men also wore white shalwar (baggy trousers with a very wide drawstring waist, tight-fitting ankles and low-flying crotch – think MC Hammer …) that were partly concealed beneath embroidered waistcoats or dark flowing overcoats. These were made of felt, reached to the calf and had wide sleeves with broad and elaborately decorated cuffs. The men chatted quietly, playing lightning-fast games of backgammon and inhaling frequently on the aromatic fumes of water pipes that sat in the midst of each group. I was amazed to see that some even wore wickedly curved jewel-handled knives or mother-of-pearl inlaid flint lock pistols tucked into their belts.

I passed through, unheeded, an incongruous interloper in cargo pants and a Rolling Stones t-shirt.

As I remember, this square and others like it were built up against the Great Umayyad Mosque that lay at the centre of the

Old City. One of the holiest sites in Islam, it is also one of the oldest mosques and, I think, one of the most beautiful in the world. Built in the seventh century, it lies on the site of an earlier Christian basilica dedicated to the most famous Damascene, John the Baptist.

After coming to a sticky end at the hands of Herod and his grand-niece/stepdaughter Salome, John's body was buried at Sebaste in Samaria, a mountainous area to the north of Jerusalem. John was imprisoned by Herod after he criticised the ruler for his incestuous marriage to his niece Herodias, which was contrary to Old Testament Law. Herodias was obviously piqued by John's vocal disapproval, because she told Salome to ask for his head as a prize for her infamous and unsavoury sexy dance for her stepdad/great-uncle.

While history is clear about the final resting place of John's body, the whereabouts of his head are less clear. But as is the way with holy relics, there is never just one. In fact, there are six heads of John the Baptist. I visited one of them at a shrine to the great man located inside the prayer hall of the Great Umayyad Mosque. Another head rests in the basilica of San Silvestro in Capite in Rome; a third is at the Residenz Museum in Munich; one used to reside in Amiens Cathedral in France; another at Antioch in Turkey; and somewhat bizarrely, there was one in the parish church at Tenterden in Kent in the UK until it disappeared during the Reformation.

The one at Amiens was pinched from Constantinople by Knight Templar Wallon de Sarton during the fourth crusade and brought to Amiens. John's head was the reason the cathedral was built, and it was installed on 17 December 1206. Subsequently lost, it was replaced by a nineteenth-century replica which, puzzlingly, is just as revered. If it's good enough for pilgrims it's good enough for me, so I've included it in the list. Archaeology isn't very good at identifying the intangible foibles of human nature. Stupidity, stubbornness, illogical superstition and downright eccentricity rarely leave clear archaeological remains, and even if it could disprove an ingrained superstition, archaeology can't always prove or disprove beliefs. And, what then? If, for example, one managed to gain access to John's heads and determine that one or possibly none of the skulls was genuinely his, would that change people's minds, diminish their beliefs? Science proved that the Turin Shroud was a medieval fake. It reassured the nonbelievers, was ignored by the devout, and the legacy of the whole hoo-ha is that a small square of cloth is missing from one corner. Some stories are best left alone.

John's are not the only mortal remains revered at the Umayyad Mosque. The great Saracen general and ruler, and a hero of mine, Saladin – or to give him his wonderful proper name, Salah al-Din Yusuf ibn Ayyub – is buried in a dedicated mausoleum in a garden outside the mosque. Saladin was a Kurd from Tikrit in northern Iraq, who rose through the ranks of the Saracen army during the twelfth-century crusades to become the sultan of an empire that stretched from North Africa to the Arabian Peninsula and the whole of the Middle East. He was the founder of the vastly influential Ayyubid Dynasty, and in his spare time recaptured Palestine and the supremely important Jerusalem. While he was the scourge of Christian invaders, his brilliance on the battlefield and his courageous and chivalrous conduct earned him respect from the crusader commanders, including Richard the Lionheart. Schooled in the arts and sciences and devastating on the field of battle, Saladin was the epitome of a medieval knight.

The crusades were a series of military campaigns that represent a two-hundred-year struggle for domination of the Holy Land during the Middle Ages. Initially, they were ideologically driven. At least, that was the official line. The Byzantine Empire had suffered significant losses to face, as well as of subjects and the profitable land of Anatolia (modern Turkey) to various Muslim armies, particularly the Seljuks. The Holy Land had been under Muslim control since the seventh century, and while Palestine had been part of the Umayyad, Abbasid and Fatimid dynasties for over three hundred years, Christian pilgrims had been able to access the sacred sites of the Holy Land.

The Seljuk campaigns in Anatolia disrupted the pilgrim routes and were one of the main reasons for Pope Urban II (no relation to Keith) to proclaim the first crusade in 1095. The stated goal was to restore and secure access to Jerusalem and the holy sites nearby. As a bit of encouragement, Urban promised forgiveness of all sins to those who took up the cross and joined in the holy and just war. Hundreds of thousands of Roman Catholics became crusaders for what some see as a war against Islamic expansion and others see as a Papal-sanctioned expansion of Western Christendom. Nine crusades can be identified between 1095 and the late thirteenth century, although they were never called crusades by the participants. The term 'crusade' was not commonly applied to the Holy Wars in the Middle East until the mid-eighteenth century, five hundred years later. Instead, the participants were variously known as the Knights of Christ or the faithful of Sancti Petri, Saint Peter.

Generally, they were a shambles and a massive headache for the places that happened to be en route. There were no coherent unifying goals, no command structure, just a vague 'Pop over Saracen side and give 'em a taste of Christian steel'. The roads between Western Europe and the Middle East must have been thick with fresh-faced zealots heading east and less enthusiastic but sin-free veterans limping west. Many went because they were told to by their feudal masters. All required food and shelter and many took these by force from the unfortunate communities along the way.

Rome didn't care. Urban's decision to declare war on the Muslims and his clever and propagandist preachings proved extremely popular. A wave of pious anger rolled over Europe, unifying the Roman Catholic church and ensuring its dominance not only as the European church but also as the predominant political and economic force of the time. Of course, religious zealotry defaults to intolerance, barbarism and, ironically in this case, lots of sinful behaviour. European Jews were massacred by crusading armies heading east who reasoned that they may as well include the supposed 'killers of Christ' in their terms of reference. Once in the Holy Land, there were many instances where 'no quarter' (no mercy) was given and whole villages, towns and cities were put to the sword. On entering Jerusalem for the first time in 1099, the crusading army killed everyone in the city and set most of it on fire.

The litany of crimes continued, culminating in the sacking of Constantinople (Istanbul) during the fourth crusade. Many citizens were butchered and the city looted. It scandalised Rome, and Pope Innocent III, who had initiated part four of the Holy War franchise, ex-communicated the crusaders. But it was too late. This action ensured that the schism between the Western and Eastern churches would never be repaired. It wasn't until 2001 that Pope John Paul II expressed sorrow and offered an apology to the leaders of the Eastern Orthodox church. (Horse. Bolted.)

The only good that came out of two centuries of pointless brutality are the extraordinary castles that survive across the eastern Mediterranean and Middle East, and I was going to see one of the best.

*

I could have spent weeks wandering the narrow lanes that travelled in and out of the past and through legend and myth, but my dig was in the remote northern desert, so with regret I left Damascus. I was meeting the rest of the dig team in Aleppo. I waved goodbye to my secret policemen and caught the bus for the all-day journey north.

By early evening I was checking into one of the greatest hotels in this part of the world, the Baron Hotel, downtown Aleppo. From the outside it's an unassuming block of a building, three storeys high with Moorish arched windows and chunky balconies on the first floor hemmed with wrought iron balustrades. I recall it wasn't particularly comfy, the beds were terrible and rooms musty, but the history was astounding. The Baron is the oldest hotel in Syria and was built by the Armenian Masloumain brothers around 1909 in expansive gardens on the outskirts of Aleppo. The story goes that the gardens were once so big that guests could shoot game, including hyena, from the hotel terrace while enjoying a cocktail. For many years it was the only place for foreigners to stay, and until the 1940s it entertained mainly British and German guests. The Berlin-to-Baghdad railway passed through Aleppo so you could imagine the scene: while the First World War raged in Europe, British archaeologist spies glowered darkly across the smoke-hazed hotel bar at cocktail-swilling Germans cavorting with their fez-wearing friends.

After the war the railway was divided up by the British and others and completed to connect Europe via Istanbul with Baghdad. In the interwar period it became the most impossibly romantic and luxurious railway in the world, the Orient–Taurus

Express. One of the main overnight stops was Aleppo, and the Baron was the destination of choice for the rich and famous who wanted to experience the exotic Near East from the comfort of a Pullman coach.

I was met in the foyer by an elderly gentleman at the modest reception desk. He turned out to be a son of one of the original Armenian owners, and he asked me to register my details in a thick and well-thumbed ledger. He then flicked the pages towards the front and with a puffed-out chest showed me the names of some of the illustrious guests of the past. It turned out that this was the original hotel register and my name now lies with the likes of Agatha Christie, Theodore Roosevelt, Kemal Ataturk, the Rockefellers, Amelia Earhart, Charles de Gaulle and Lawrence of Arabia. There were their signatures, and as I looked around the faded opulence of the lobby, I saw other remnants of those adventurous and glamorous times. Above the polished and cracked Chesterfield sofas, the faded original posters advertising the Orient Express adorned the walls.

I felt a bit faded too after my travels, so I headed to the cocktail bar and ordered a martini (I may be a Bond fan but a well-made martini is extraordinary). I was too embarrassed to ask for it shaken, but it was very good and very, very strong. I have a vivid memory of that night. The evening was balmy, and I was sunk into an old leather club chair on the terrace, head thrown back, listening to the call to prayer and languidly smoking while the third martini unscrewed the top of my head. I remember thinking that this was exactly where I wanted my life to be at that moment. I was twenty-one and I was living an adventure.

I wrote in a diary once, I think when I was about twelve or thirteen, that I was going to be an adventurer like Allan Quatermain or Indiana Jones. It was one of those simple, matter-of-fact statements that kids make because they are yet to encounter the crippling burden of self-doubt. That night I really felt I had lived up to that dream.

There are a number of places in the world where you can feel history thick in the air, where you sense that you are standing at a focal point in the human story, which is thrilling for archaeologists. I've always thought strongly that London has that feeling and undoubtedly Jerusalem, Damascus and Istanbul do too. Aleppo also felt like that and I loved it. I had a day in town before I had to meet up with the team. So I explored the old city without the fetters of secret police.

Aleppo is the largest city in Syria and historically one of the most important cities in the Middle East, with a history reaching back thousands of years. But the monument that dominates and defines it, the Citadel, dates to the twelfth and thirteenth centuries. It's an extraordinary pile of masonry that rises almost one hundred metres above the old walled city. It is one of the largest and oldest castles in the world and testament to the military might of the Arabs. Even to the modern eye that is used to huge feats of engineering, the scale of the Citadel is astounding. The imposing mound is surrounded by a massive moat, twenty-five metres deep and thirty metres wide, and is lined, as are the sides of the mound, with giant slabs of limestone. The battlements at the summit enclose an oval space four hundred metres long by over three hundred wide. Over the two hundred years and countless attacks of the crusader campaigns, neither the Citadel nor Aleppo were taken from the Arab forces, and in fact a number of famous crusaders were imprisoned here, including Baldwin II (possibly related to Alec, after all, he is Alexander Baldwin III), the King of Jerusalem.

The Citadel is noted as the final resting place of St George, the patron saint of England, one of the most important figures in Christianity. There is a shrine in the castle dedicated to St George, and I stood at the foot of a green cloth-draped tomb wondering how such a very English figure ended up in this dusty room. Of course, like a lot of things that the English consider their own – think tea (Chinese), chicken tikka masala (Scottish – no, really), ale (Belgian) and bad weather (Irish) – St George wasn't English at all; he was Greek. So what was he doing in Aleppo?

The story goes that St George was a crusader who died in battle in the Holy Land in the twelfth century. Unfortunately for the crusader story, St George died a regulation horrible death as an early Christian martyr on 23 April 303, eight hundred years before the first crusade. A prominent and respected soldier in the Roman army, St George of Lydda achieved the position of tribune and was a member of the imperial guard for Emperor Diocletian. He was, however, a Christian, and even after Diocletian himself implored him to renounce his beliefs, he refused and was tortured and decapitated. His body was returned to his home town of Lydda, now named Lod, near Ben Gurion Airport in Israel, nowhere near Aleppo.

While the occupant of the tomb in the Citadel is anyone's guess, it seems the St George connection with the crusades and patronage with England arose with the popularity of the story of George's martyrdom in the eastern Byzantine Empire during the time of the crusades. George's strength of faith and his warrior background appealed to the crusading soldiers, who brought the story and his symbol (a red cross on a white background) back to England. While it's often the case, I do find it annoying that facts always seem to get in the way of a great story.

The terrible Syrian Civil War being waged at present is exacting an unforgivable toll on innocent Syrians and is also having a terrible impact on the nation's cherished cultural heritage. The Citadel has been damaged by mortar and artillery fire, and one of my seriously favourite places on the planet, the Aleppo Souk, has been destroyed. It was the most wonderful labyrinth of narrow cobbled laneways covered with stone barrel-vaulted roofs. Slanting blue columns of light pierced the gloom through holes in the vaults, highlighting smoke from barbecues and water pipes, powdered spices and the dust of centuries. It was loud and crowded, colourful and totally, brilliantly mad. And now it's gone and Syria and the world are poorer for its loss.

*

I met up with the dig team at a rooftop restaurant in the Old City. One of my university friends, Dave, a thin, bespectacled and supremely funny Scouser from Liverpool, was there along with a dozen others, mostly students from the Oriental Institute of Chicago, Columbia University in New York City and a couple of specialists from London and Harvard.

As we seasoned diggers compared stories of projects, horrible insects and interesting diseases, the students sat sipping their sweet tea and spinning out. I'd seen it before, the frozen expression, tight-lipped smile and dilated pupils. Culture shock was hitting them like a freight train. None had been to the Middle East before. None had left the United States and one hadn't travelled beyond his home county. While not exactly smug, I did feel like a sage and worldly figure in comparison.

Twenty-four hours later, I was standing with a similarly forced smile, the dust of the departing bus settling on my face as I looked at a small huddle of huts that we would call home for the next three months. Tell es-Sweyhat lies about 160 kilometres from Aleppo, a slow four-hour drive to the north-west on the eastern side of the Euphrates. It lay in the centre of a broad, flat embayment bordered to the west by the river and to the east by a rugged escarpment that curved away to the north and south.

The village was about two kilometres south-east of the site and was literally in the middle of bloody nowhere. People generally set up home in places that are convenient to the basics: water, good soils, tasty animals, the hardware store. Our village, which didn't have a name as far as I could tell, was conveniently located in the middle of the most barren desert I have ever seen, and I've seen a lot of desert. There was no electricity (the nearest town with a supply was over fifty kilometres away), no gas, no running water or sewerage. After the bus dropped us and our bags and headed back to Aleppo, the project pick-up truck was the only motor vehicle in the village. The thirty or so buildings, the compound walls and even the chicken coops (strange beehive-shaped shelters) were mud brick.

Because there were no cars, there were no streets and the village layout seemed ad hoc and alien. No power poles or telephone lines interrupted the horizon, and it was quiet apart from the occasional bray of a donkey or the call of a rooster. I had lived in remote places before but never where there was no vegetation, not a scrubby bush, not a field, not a blade of grass. Most of the homes had vegetable gardens, but they were hidden from view behind mud-brick walls. So for months my world was sandy beige and sky blue.

We were shown to our billets, which turned out to be spare mud-brick huts dotted around the village. A small compound on the northern edge of the settlement contained the work rooms, meal hut, kitchen and toilets. 'Toilet' is perhaps a generous term, but I'm not sure what to call a huge hole in the ground under a chair with the seat knocked out of it, balanced precariously on two bouncy planks that spanned the six-foot drop. Trips to the loo were intense, and after a couple of days, frequent. Our driver also doubled as the cook, which was a pity, because he was a terrible driver and he couldn't cook. His personal hygiene was non-existent and seemingly his food hygiene was worse.

Tell es-Sweyhat, as the name suggests, is a large tell. 'Tell' is an archaeological term for an artificial mound made up of hundreds, sometimes thousands, of layers of remains of human occupation, comprising mostly demolition rubble and rubbish. Over thousands of years communities of people have built, demolished and built again on these sites, causing the mounds to rise above the surrounding landscape. The longer and more intense the occupation history, the larger the mound. Tells are found throughout the Middle East and Turkey (where they are called *tepes* or *höyüks*) but especially along the flood plains and ancient irrigation lands of the Euphrates and the Tigris rivers. There are thousands of them, rising sometimes up to one hundred metres above the plains and covering hundreds of hectares, each clear evidence that this now barren, dusty landscape was once anything but.

The mystery of what happened to these communities was one of the reasons we found ourselves in the middle of nowhere in the autumn of 1991. Earlier excavations at the site in the 1970s had showed that it was a modest village in the beginning, but by the Early Bronze Age it had grown in size and influence to become one of the main settlements and powers of the region.

As we know, the Bronze Age was the period of human prehistory that stretched between 3300 and 1200 BC, when the copper alloy bronze was produced for the first time and used extensively. While it is useful in broadly categorising human development through technological advances, the term fails to capture the monumental developments across the board that occurred during this era. Following on from the shift from hunter-gathering to farming, as seen in the Neolithic, communities became more complex. With so much effort tied up in agricultural pursuits, farmers were time-poor when it came to other needs. The result was an increase in the number and diversity of specialist jobs that provided the early farmers with goods such as pots and wheels and buildings. The administration of society became multi-streamed and sophisticated. And the Middle East, specifically the area known as the Fertile Crescent, was the beginning of it all.

The Fertile Crescent is a nineteenth-century term coined to describe the crescent-shaped region stretching from Upper Egypt across the Levantine countries of Jordan, Israel, Palestine, Lebanon and Syria, and east and south across southern Turkey and down the vast river plains of the Euphrates and Zagros. When Tell es-Sweyhat was a bustling town, the foundations of those pillars of modern society, politics, judiciary, commerce and education, were in place. Writing was codified – in this area it was cuneiform. Writing facilitated and recorded the trade of food and effort. But, just as importantly, it allowed the exposition and dissemination of ideas. The invention of the wheel both expanded trade and saw the development for the first time of mass-produced goods through the potter's wheel.

It's one of the most important eras of human history, and the crumbling ruins of mud-brick buildings and broken pottery that we uncovered were humble evidence of this extraordinary time. But all I knew on the first morning, as I stood shivering on the top of the tell, was that I didn't have enough warm clothing. At midday the mercury rose to uncomfortable levels, but even though it was only mid-October, the desert climate saw the night temperatures drop dramatically to near freezing.

It was as I was jumping around, trying to get feeling in my toes, that I noticed a dust cloud in the distance to the north-east. Someone pointed to another coming from the north-west and a third from the direction of the village we were staying in a couple of kilometres away from the Tell. Out of the dust emerged people on donkeys – lots and lots of people, and they were heading straight for us. We all stood flabbergasted as over a hundred locals, men, women and children, stopped at the foot of the tell, dismounted from their stumpy steeds and waited expectantly. They were our workforce and I had just stepped back forty years to a time when archaeological sites were dug by a cast of hundreds.

I recall thinking, *Great, I'm fresh out of university, I'm in the middle of nowhere, digging a site I know nothing about, with a bunch of workers who don't know how to dig, and who haven't a clue what I'm saying.* I stomped off to a point about fifty metres north of the base of the tell, to an area suspected to be the outer, or lower, town, and perhaps twenty locals trailed after me. They ranged in age from six to perhaps seventy, although it was difficult to tell because the desert life ages people quickly. They were a pretty amiable bunch who soon got into the rhythm of the dig, and they all thought I was completely mad. They understood the digging up of artefacts, they kind of got our interest in the mud-brick ruins, but they couldn't handle why we dug so slowly. When they heard that the trench would be backfilled at the end of the season only to be dug up again the following year, they shook their heads and wandered off.

I was named the Writing Man from all the notes that I made, and I guess they felt sorry for me trying to write while shivering uncontrollably in the mornings. After a brief whispered discussion, they set two of the young lads first thing every day to gather up the droppings (of which there was a growing pile) from where the donkeys were tethered for the day and make a dung fire at my feet. They were nice people with a lot of laughter and who used to wind each other up with a familiarity common to small and isolated communities.

The women here seemed to have greater liberty than I'd seen in other rural areas of the Middle East. While their dress was modest and traditional, it was clear that they called the shots and ran the communities. They moved around the dig head-to-toe in black multi-layered gowns. Their headscarves were beautifully patterned silk, universally black, with deep red swirls. They wore black shalwahs (trousers) with a full-length black dress and cape over the top. The older women showed their faces and exhibited tattoos that looked like stylised beards on their chins, which in many instances, I was told, was exactly what they were. If a community elder's wife was widowed and she wished or was obliged to take on her late husband's role, she often adopted a stylised beard as a nod to the preferred gender for such roles. I asked once why they didn't have tattooed moustaches as well, and they looked at me like I was a fool and told me: 'Because it would look silly.'

The younger women on site generally preferred to cover their faces, leaving just their eyes exposed. One woman in my team had the most beautiful kohl-framed sky-blue eyes. They were mesmerising and they seemed to be on me whenever I looked in her direction. She gazed at me without embarrassment and often sent me flushed and flustered, stumbling up the tell to the trench of my mate Dave, who was having uncomfortable moments of his own with the women of the desert. Whereas I was getting the eye, he was getting an eyeful. He came flying down the mound one day at a full run and skidded to a halt at my fire.

'Jesus Christ,' he said, raking his trembling hand through his black hair. 'Jesus Christ, Adam, you've got to protect me.'

I smiled but he looked genuinely scared. He explained that he'd been busy recording part of his dig when one of the women on his team called his name. 'I turned around and Whidad, you know, the younger one, had her top pulled up and she wiggled her naked breasts at me.'

'You're kidding,' I said.

'No really, and then they all laughed and then the old girls started whispering and pointing and sort of miming putting on rings.' He paused and looked at me. 'I think they're fitting me up to marry Whidad!'

I fell to the ground laughing while he swore at me.

After that, I tried to avoid Blue Eyes.

*

The excavation was quite complex: the challenge was to differentiate surviving mud-brick structures from the mass of collapsed and dissolved mud bricks and soil in which they were buried. The soil, being the same stuff that the mud bricks were made of, was therefore the same colour as both the surviving mud bricks and the collapsed and decayed mud bricks. My dreams were inhabited by beige mud bricks. Essentially, I was guided by slight differences in compaction of the deposits, with the surviving mud-brick walls marginally more compact than the overlying collapsed bricks. To start with this was a bit nerve-racking, but I soon got my eye in and started to enjoy the dig.

This Bronze Age city in its heyday would have been about five hundred metres across, with a tightly packed huddle of houses, protected by a perimeter wall and overlooked by a citadel rising above all on the tell mound. Resting for thousands of years less than a half a metre below the desert surface were the ruins of a temple that served the community of Tell es-Sweyhat in the fourth and third millennium BC (3100 to 1900 BC). Running alongside the outer wall of the temple, a narrow lane gave a glimpse of the urban landscape, similar to the little lanes between the mud-brick houses in our village a mile or so to the south-east. But the large open interior spaces, with wide and well-made stone wall foundations, indicated this building was of higher status than the domestic dwellings found elsewhere on site, or indeed in the village. It was the statues that were a bit of a giveaway about the function of the building. Approximately six inches high, numerous clay figurines were discovered scattered across the floor of the temple. Each was different and each had a name inscribed on the shoulder; it is probable that they were surrogates for devotees who were unable to attend the temple.

While this was interesting, I found the artefacts and architecture of domestic spaces even more fascinating, as they were a dusty window onto a way of life five thousand years ago that was part understandable and part impossible to comprehend. It was halfway through the dig that one of our neighbours in the compound started building a wing onto his house. I followed the process with increasing interest. He began by taking stone from an abandoned building on the other side of the village and using it to form a dry-stone foundation wall. Onto this he built up the lower wall by laying the stones in a herringbone pattern, mortared with clay. This was then rendered and the upper walls were raised further with mud brick. It was interesting in itself to get an insight into construction that was so alien to European building, but it was all the more amazing when we recognised the method as the same employed by the occupants of the site five thousand years before. The construction was identical. Talk about if it ain't broke …

Why the ancient settlement was abandoned remains a mystery. Some scholars attribute over-irrigation and subsequent increased soil salinity to the collapse of the extraordinary societies that lined the Euphrates from Turkey to the Arabian Gulf. Others point to the complex but seemingly inevitable collapse of empires that have occurred throughout history. It could have been disease, or climate change, or a mix of all the above. Maybe one day we can go back to that troubled part of the world and find out.

The dig may have been a challenge, but everything was made a whole lot worse thanks to the cook. I'd become sick within days of arriving. We all had, to varying degrees. Physically it wasn't that bad: gut cramps mainly, not enough to stop you working. It was just a constant discomfort, mixed with a sweat-inducing fear that wore you down: the ever-present fear of crapping yourself. Then one day near the end of the dig, that fear went away, and not because I got better.

I had worked out that, from the first warning cramps, I had just enough time to grab my bag (which always contained a loo roll), mince my way around the base of the mound and make it to the toilet trenches, a distance of perhaps three hundred metres. These were the deep archaeological trenches excavated in the 1970s that afforded the only privacy in the desolate landscape. On this occasion I had wasted precious seconds searching for my bloody bag, which lay hidden under an upturned bucket, and, as

I made my way, clenched against the tempest within, my heart sank as I knew I wasn't going to make it. I felt the eyes of the team following me.

I had two options and both were bleak. I could shit myself, which was not a big deal necessarily, considering I had done so on a number of occasions thanks to various bugs in the three years I'd been working in the Middle East. But these were my last pair of pants, all the others had fallen apart, and I would have to waddle the two kilometres back to the village to wash. Or I could drop my pants in front of everyone and suffer devastating public humiliation of the first order.

I dropped my pants. I was out of laundry powder.

I squatted with my trousers around my ankles, and as the sun beat down on my skinny white behind, I violently evacuated. 'Oh no. No, no, no, no,' I remember muttering bitterly through dirty fingers as I cradled my face.

Eighty or so friends, fellow archaeologists and local villagers looked on from the ancient mound behind me. My face burned as I imagined the sight I was presenting to them all. Laughter, clapping and whoops of glee reached my bright red ears across the two hundred metres of sand and rock.

'Total bastards!' I shouted over my shoulder.

Eventually, I stood on shaky legs and turned to face my tormentors. The whole dig team stood on the dusty hill above me, silhouetted against the fierce afternoon sun. I raised my arms above my head and gave a double two-finger salute to them all.

The team cheered loudly, waving shovels in the air. Mustafa, the site guard, fired a dozen shots into the air from his beaten-up AK-47. I reluctantly bowed to the audience, exited stage left and stomped off, back to the village to wash my hands.

*

With no transport, no bus service and only one day off a week, spare time was restricted to sleeping, laundry and writing up notes. The directors were old school, meaning that they thought long hours, discomfort, isolation and crap food was all part of archaeology. It is a unique experience to be thrown together with a bunch of strangers (most of us barely out of our teens), often from different parts of the world, in difficult and isolated conditions for months on end. It is not easy and it's not for everyone; and it cannot be underestimated how awful things can get if someone (our friend on the Wadi Fidan project springs to mind) is unable to keep it together.

Considering the disparate nature of the Sweyhat team, the project held together well and even the most culture-shocked and homesick began to enjoy the experience. Even so, squabbles inevitably crept into the dig house. But an incident near the end of the project silenced our petty sniping.

Word got to us one day from the neighbouring village that a small boy, about six years old, had fallen down one of the narrow wells that dotted the settlements. A rescue was being carried out but hopes of reaching the child were not high. Of course, we were upset and arranged for one of the directors to drive into Manjib, the nearest town, or Aleppo to get help. We knew it was unlikely that help would arrive until the next day and we tried our best to stay focused on the dig and not think of the poor kid jammed in a narrow dark hole in the ground. The feeling on site was terrible and the villagers were either in tears or quiet. We heard that the boy was calling for help and that his family was holding a vigil at the mouth of the well, uttering such words of encouragement that they could find.

Help didn't arrive the next day or the one following. I have never felt so inadequate. We had neither the expertise or equipment to assist. When I thought about the poor lad I felt physically sick. Apparently he was about ten metres down, too injured or squeezed to hold a rope. Time was running out and we sat in silence during the long evenings. About midnight on the third night Phil, the director, returned with the driver. He looked awful and in tears told us that no one either in Manjib or Aleppo was able or willing to help. No one was coming. The villagers took the news with silent resignation and rallied around the boy's family and community as best they could.

Seven days after falling into the well, the lad stopped calling out, and the following day the well was filled in.

I recovered from my public humiliation, but the death of the young boy had a profound effect on me, and it was with mixed emotions that I sat in the back of the truck and watched the village disappear in a cloud of dust. There is a strange feeling of sadness that comes with leaving these projects. It's such an intense and all-consuming experience that you never leave the same person as you arrived, and it often takes weeks or longer to get back into normal life. I can only imagine what it is like for service personnel and aid workers returning from conflict. All the same, I was tired and wanted to go home. I wanted my own space, I wanted to sit on a proper loo and I desperately wanted some cheddar cheese.

I travelled back to Damascus to spend a couple of days Christmas shopping before heading home. Weary after the months up north on the dig and being ill for such a long time, I sat with a considerable amount of relief at a little restaurant in downtown Damascus at the western edge of the Old City. I wasn't followed on this visit, so either it had been decided that I was no threat to the regime or they didn't want to catch my stomach bug. I hailed the waiter and asked for a Barada beer, some peanuts, and a mezze for one. I remember this meal very well. It tasted fantastic and I have been waxing lyrical about it for twenty years. Everything combined to make such a simple feed, by oneself in a small restaurant on a busy street in a mad city, perfect. This meal, the kebabs I had in Shuna in northern Jordan and the amazing falafel rolls in Jerusalem explain my lifelong love affair with Middle Eastern and Mediterranean food. The beer was a strange green colour and had a mellow woody taste (both provided by olive-wood barrels). It was unusual but tasted like nectar of the gods compared to the dodgy Al-Shark beer of Aleppo (a strong suspect in my equally dodgy gut problem).

My enjoyment turned to confusion when all of a sudden the road outside cleared of the constant horn-blaring crazy traffic. I looked at my watch, it was just gone seven. Something was going on because there were no cars at all. Irrationally, but perhaps not so on reflection, I panicked, thinking that something was very wrong. Was Syria suddenly at war? Perhaps there was an imminent airstrike of the capital and everyone knew apart from me? Well, me and all the other diners at all the restaurants along the street (that idea was falling apart as I conjured it). Worse still, had President Assad had gone completely bonkers and ordered martial law and there was a curfew? As a breaker of said curfew was I going to be arrested before my second beer? I quickly raised my hand and ordered another Barada.

Then drums started up somewhere out of sight around the corner, and a very loud and distorted shouting blared from dozens of Tannoy speakers which I noticed had been strung up on wires between the trees along the roadway. I couldn't understand what was being said but it didn't feel threatening so I sat back, swigged at my beer and watched.

Within moments a huge procession of thousands of uniformed people, each frantically waving little Syrian flags and shiny pictures of Assad, came marching round the corner in a well-rehearsed parade. Adults and children in dark-green army fatigues marched, singing and clutching their little flags.

It all seemed very jolly and impressive. I asked the waiter what was going on, and he explained with the help of a young Syrian student who had good English that this was a rehearsal for Assad's re-election celebrations. 'Oh,' I said, surprised, 'when was the vote?' I knew I'd been out in the sticks but this was the first I'd heard about a general election.

'Next month,' said the student with a completely straight face.

I forgot to catch up with 'Our Man in Damascus' before I left the next day for England and a Christmas at home. So to the British government, for your information the village didn't have a telephone or a post office or a school teacher.

And as for the price of tomatoes? They grew their own.

OF DESERT SNOWSTORMS, CAMEL SPIDERS AND INDIANA JONES ADVENTURES

However, about a year after the pharaoh had returned to Egypt,
the city of Tanis was consumed by the desert in a sandstorm,
which lasted a whole year. Wiped clean by the wrath of God.

Marcus Brody, *Raiders of the Lost Ark*, 1981

I have lived and worked at the earth's extremes of temperature, from the blistering heat of summer in the Australian bush to the deep freeze of a British summer holiday. But amazingly, both the hottest and coldest conditions I have experienced were in Jordan. (Suffering in the elements added to the adventure but that appeal is fading as I get older.)

During the Wadi Fidan project, daytime temperatures often exceeded fifty degrees Celsius. I will never know how hot it got there because our thermometers all broke, but I remember the toll the heat took on our bodies. In an effort to beat it, the workday started at four in the morning with the director shining a bright torch in our faces and, in an irritating singsong voice, saying, 'Wakey-wakey, sleeping beauties.' Every morning. There are so many experiences that have helped forge my life, both professional and private, and the director of the Wadi Fidan project is one of those standout experiences. He could have written the textbook on how not to run an archaeological project, and I believe he has made me a better director by the example of his awful leadership.

We would stumble on site to be rewarded by witnessing the first rays of sun setting the shattered hills of the Holy Land on fire. All too quickly the shadow of the ridge would shrink back from the valley floor and we would be exposed to the full force of the Middle Eastern summer sun. By eight in the morning, the heat was uncomfortable and sweat would sting your eyes and fall onto the dusty ground to evaporate as you watched with dulling senses. By ten, our work rate had slowed and it felt like someone was bludgeoning us to death with a foam mattress. By noon, we were done. Like zombies, we stumbled around the camp trying to find shade. The concrete school was stifling, so we would roll up against the base of walls in the narrow shadows of early afternoon. We even looked like zombies. The air is so dry in the summer in the valley that sweat evaporated off our skin leaving a fine dusting of salt and made our hair stick out stiffly in funky styles.

No matter how hard you tried, you couldn't get enough water into your body, and so we all suffered from dehydration, resulting in many of us, including me, getting sick. I lost ten kilograms in twelve weeks (Michelle Bridges would be proud – except most of it was out of my behind).

But when I returned to Jordan in January 1991, after a brief break back home for Christmas, I was confronted with a raw, chill wind that scudded across the dull, brown desert. I was completely unprepared. Even though the Christmas period in the UK had been freezing, I didn't imagine that it would ever get properly cold in Jordan. In fact, I had been gently winding up my friends over a farewell pint that I was once more heading back to the heat, while they had the worst of the winter to endure.

I stood shivering in downtown Amman, together, it seemed, with the whole of the capital's population. Amman sits at an elevation of about one thousand metres, so it is not unheard of for its residents to wake up on a winter morning to frosts. But I remember that day it felt like it could snow. In just a t-shirt and light cotton cargo pants, I made a beeline for the markets and picked up a load of army surplus shirts, jumpers, a padded waistcoat and heavy jacket as well as gloves, a hat and a couple of the distinctive black and white checked keffiyehs as scarves.

Bundled up, I headed back to the American Center of Oriental Research (ACOR) to meet up with a bunch of guys from the prehistory program at Arizona State University. The director was the highly regarded and all-round great chap Geoff Clark. We were due to head down to the hillside town of Tafilah, about three hours' drive south of Amman, the following day, but we woke to find Amman covered in a thick blanket of snow and a fierce blizzard adding to it at an alarming rate. What started as disbelieving shakes of the head and snowball fights in the ACOR compound turned into a tedious, sometimes uncomfortable and occasionally dangerous month, during which time the director, Geoff, became more morose and the team became more disbelieving.

The snowstorm lasted for almost a week; it was the coldest and snowiest winter on record. Images beamed around the world showed snow covering Jerusalem and the Dome of the Rock. We were just fortunate that for the first two weeks we were trapped in some of the most comfortable and well-heated buildings in Amman. But Jordan is ill-equipped to deal with such an extreme event and all but the most major roads in the city remained snowbound. Roads, including the highways out of Amman, were either impassable or dangerous, and there was no good prospect of getting to Tafilah, which lay in a mountainous section of southern Jordan.

On the occasional forays to the local shops, we watched the poor Jordanians picking their way through the thigh-deep snow. The average day for a Muslim involves removing your shoes a dozen times or more – entering mosques, people's houses etc. So slip-ons are ubiquitous. These proved to be less than ideal in the snow, and when the thaw eventually arrived, thousands of shoes were found clogging the drains and gutters. One can only think that many of the locals we saw arrived at their destinations with very wet and very cold feet.

So we played cards and exchanged stories and read books, and the snow continued to fall.

Eventually, a break in the weather unfortunately presented us with an opportunity to make it down to Tafilah. I say unfortunately because while we made it into the town and settled into our dig house with relative ease, the weather closed in behind us and we were stuck for another two weeks in a draughty concrete block house that was uninsulated and unheated. Safe to say it was the coldest two weeks I have ever experienced. The two small paraffin heaters could do nothing to ward off the bone-aching cold, and there were days when everyone stayed huddled in their beds, fully clothed.

Twice we tried to get back to Amman, but the roads had disappeared under huge drifts. During one escape attempt, we crawled behind a bulldozer that was trying to push a path through the massive snowdrifts on the mountain road. The tyres on the two Toyota Hiluxes we were driving were bald, which was making the journey comically hazardous. Movement of the steering wheel was suggestive at best of the direction we wanted to go in and seemed to have no influence on which part of the vehicle went first. We seemed to spend more time travelling sideways or rear first. But if we were having an interesting time, it was nothing on the poor guys operating the bulldozer. The blizzard was ferocious, with snow whipping sideways across the road in a roaring whiteout. And the dozer had an open cab. Well, actually, no cab. A team truck followed the slow progress of the bulldozer, and about every fifteen minutes, a guy bundled up in about twenty layers of polyester robes, shirts and light summer coats jumped out, prised the driver free of the steering wheel and sent him to the truck to thaw out. He would then freeze himself to the vehicle for the next quarter of an hour. We kept going like this for a couple of hours, but the weather was getting worse and the light was failing. Then we realised that the road behind us had disappeared. With the panic levels rising by the minute, we turned around and started to head back to Tafilah. It was touch and go but we made it back, cold and frustrated.

Geoff poked his head out of the swaddle of blankets that he was permanently under and declaimed that the Lord had at last come to punish him and we were all going to die. While I had thought the weather tough, all the others including Geoff were from Arizona, and they were not coping very well at all.

Then almost as quickly as the blizzards had rolled in, a rapid thaw saw the roads clear over a couple of days and at last we could consider starting the project.

*

The Wadi Hasa is a large valley that runs east–west from the Jordanian plateau, slicing through the rugged escarpment of the eastern side of the Jordan Valley and flowing out at the southern end of the Dead Sea at the salt town of Safi. Hundreds of thousands of years ago, erosion by the watercourse cut into the edge of a large shallow lake at the eastern end of the Hasa River on the desert plateau, draining it of its contents in what would have been an impressive flood. The aim of our project was to walk the ancient shoreline of this lake in search of archaeological sites. In the past, as now, one of the prerequisites of human settlement was fresh water. So while the survey area was now dry and inhospitable, in ancient times it would have been a lush and sustaining environment.

The snow had mostly melted but the desert plateau remained cold, and we stomped up and down these dry shorelines bundled up in everything we could wear. We found amazing sites everywhere, ranging from rock shelter encampments, which dated back a quarter of a million years, to Ottoman forts and historic Bedouin burials.

The country was bleak and Martian-like but we all grew very fond of it. There is something greatly relaxing about simply wandering slowly through a landscape. You have time to really look around, to read the landforms and imagine what it was like in the past. One of the greatest skills for an archaeologist, one that works in the field anyway, is the ability to look beyond what you see in front of you and to imagine how it was in the past. What opportunities or challenges did it present to our ancestors? Where would be the best place to camp, to traverse the land or to hunt for food?

One book more than all others has impressed on me, as a field archaeologist, the importance of being able to read the landscape to understand the past. *The Making of the English Landscape* was written by WG Hoskins in the 1950s. Hoskins was a historian and he described how, when looked at in the right way, the English landscape gives evidence of its past like a huge pop-up history book. He said, 'One needs to be a botanist, a physical geographer, and a naturalist, as well as a historian to understand a scene in full.'

Quite quickly at Wadi Hasa I began to see the subtle features that showed the edge of the ancient lake shoreline where a spring may have been, or the most likely location for a seasonal camp. Sure enough, we discovered sites in these areas and they provided ample evidence that this inhospitable desert was once a vegetated landscape, providing enough food and resources to support small communities in semi-permanent camps.

Over three months we recorded hundreds of sites and also discovered over a hundred flip-flops. Strangely, 90 per cent were for the left foot.

The method of survey was quite simple. We spread out in a line with about ten metres between each team member. Guided by compasses, we walked transects of about four kilometres long, then turned around and walked a parallel transect. Clearly, only a portion of the landscape was viewed, so it was more remarkable that we discovered two halves of the same Ottoman-era cannonball, which lay over a kilometre apart.

*

Our commute in two twin-cab Hilux pick-ups to the survey area took us past the small town of Hasa. A week into the project, we were pulled over by a police officer who waved us to the side of the highway. With lots of staring and a bit of tutting, he examined my international driver's permit and that of the guy driving the other vehicle.

We explained who we were and what we were doing, and normally at the mention of *athar* ('archaeologist' in Arabic), you would be greeted with smiles or at least sympathy. But in this case, he shrugged, confiscated our licences and told us not to drive with our lights on. I looked around. It was foggy and the sun had just risen, but it was still quite dull. We got out and swapped drivers and continued on our way.

The next morning we were pulled over again. Again, the driver's licences were taken, this time for *not* having our headlights on. We were running out of drivers but couldn't work out what was going on. If they wanted a bit of kickback cash, they hadn't made it very clear, and the last thing we wanted was to be charged with trying to bribe a police officer. So we changed drivers again and headed off to work. Two days later they were waiting for us again and without even being beckoned we pulled over. The drivers handed over their permits and without a word we changed drivers. Twice more over the following week we were stopped, until we were down to the last two drivers. Geoff had had enough and marched off to the Tafilah post office to make a call back to ACOR in Amman.

At that time ACOR enjoyed the patronage of Queen Noor, wife of King Hussein (father of the current monarch, King Abdullah II), and of the gently spoken and genial Prince Ra'ad bin Zeid, who was at the time Minister of the Interior and was a cousin of His Majesty. He is also head of the royal houses of Iraq and Syria.

Unbeknown to us, the head of ACOR called the Prince about our trouble with the Hasa fuzz. The following day, the whole of the Hasa police station was waiting in full uniform and standing at attention. They waved us to a stop with massive forced smiles on their faces, came and shook our hands and handed back our documents. Clearly, Prince Ra'ad had had a word, apparently personally to the police chief. Every day after that we were greeted with enthusiastic waves and smiles as we passed the Hasa township.

Quite often we bumped into Bedouin during the survey, and a few times we were invited to their huge black goat-hair tents for some tea and a bit of a chat. The language issue meant that these chats were an elaborate game of charades liberally punctuated with repeated 'how are you', 'nice to meet you', 'hello', 'thank you very much', 'good' or 'very good'. It also provided an opportunity for the women to grab the girls on the team, giggle at their bedraggled hair and ask them about bras and knickers. Surprisingly, it seemed that the Bedouin women were fascinated by what western women wore under their outer clothes.

For the guys, we sat around with the heads of the families, nodded a lot and made suitably impressed noises at the collection of treasures and weapons that were brought out for us to look at. They were friendly and hospitable people, generous with their time and their super sweet tea, and were for the most part comfortably off compared to many in Jordanian society. Some were a bit too eager to shoot their machine guns into the air, but they were a proud bunch with a long and amazing heritage, as evidenced by their curved swords and flintlock rifles, handed down no doubt by their forefathers, who had fought the Ottomans and others. Many of the Jordanian Bedouin had been instrumental in the Arab Revolt during the First World War.

Unfortunately, two of the younger American women on the project team who had never travelled before saw the dirt and the tents and the slightly tatty clothes and interpreted it as poverty. They took it upon themselves to give the Bedouin a helping hand. Culture shock comes in many guises, but perhaps the most annoying and embarrassing for all concerned is misguided benevolence. One evening while we were sorting and cataloguing stone artefacts, they unpacked a strange assortment of odds and ends that they had bought from the shop; lighters, pens, pencils, little snacks, novelty erasers. They laid them out in piles and started putting them into bags.

When asked what they were doing, they explained that they were 'Bedouin gift packs'.

I looked blankly at the other team members, who blinked back at me.

'What are they for?' I asked.

'Well, they are so poor,' they said, looking outraged that I hadn't noticed.

'And a pencil and a rubber will help?' I said. I didn't know whether to laugh or cry.

Apparently, I didn't understand. The others wisely kept their mouths shut, and so I was the focus of the women's fury against the unjust world around us. With these kits the noble Bedouin (their words) could use the lighter to light fires! They could have a snack while tending their sheep and perhaps write a letter or sketch their noble lands ...

I gave up and went to bed.

The following week we bumped into some of the guys we'd had tea with a couple of weeks before. After saying hello a couple of times and sharing some smokes, we showed them a Bedouin grave that we had discovered. It had been dug up recently and the bones of the occupant had been flung all round the grave. The Bedouin guys stood there and the eldest shot a quick glance at two younger herders, who were looking a bit sheepish. It was not unusual for graves to be dug up like this in search of treasure and it appeared that the young lads had been shaking down their ancestors.

Just then the two girls came hurrying over, clutching their Bedouin gift packs. The others and I only had enough time to say sorry before the excruciating gift ceremony played out before us.

Bewildered, the men took the proffered bags and opened them up. Briefly peering inside, they looked at each other and then at us. I shrugged and mouthed, 'I'm sorry,' again.

They didn't know what to say. Formal gift-giving is quite tricky and can often create an awkward situation where the recipient may feel obliged to give back at the equivalent value or status. But in this case they didn't know what the hell was going on. Unfortunately, their silence was interpreted as noble gratification and the two do-gooders looked at me, vindicated, and strutted off.

The eldest guy followed their retreating backs then looked at us and flicked his hand palm up, a simple gesture that could only be translated as, *What was that about?*

My mate Mike, who is six foot seven, looked down at the ground briefly and tapped the side of his head, and then everyone nodded sagely.

Word must have got around, because from then on the packs were received with gracious acceptance. It was not long, however, before they were found littering the desert, complete except for the lighters.

Our cook on the Hasa project was a little old Palestinian man called Abu Joseph and it is his story, more than anything else that I saw in the Middle East, that brought home to me the nature and scale of the human tragedy that has unfolded in the region since the end of the Second World War. Abu Joseph was one of those people you would describe as spritely. I guess at the time he would have been in his mid-sixties. His hair and moustache were grey, and his thin face was weather-beaten and heavily lined, but you could still see that he would have been a good-looking chap in his prime. He was rake-thin, his clothes hung off his frame and his digital watch looked too large for his narrow wrists.

He took a shine to me because I was the only Brit in the team. He explained that he had been a cook for the British troops during the war and laughed at the memory. 'Fish and chips,' he said in his heavily accented English. 'All they want was fish and chips … fish and chips, fish and chips!' He laughed again.

Often after dinner we would sit on the roof of the drab concrete apartment we were living in and he would tell me about his life. His English was good and he seemed to enjoy using it. He had been born into a prosperous family who owned and managed a large farm on the edge of the western bank of the Jordan Valley. At that time the family farm was in Palestine, and his youth, he told me, while full of hard work on the farm, was peaceful. Then the war came and that was the end of peace for him. The battles of the Palestinian campaign came and went, and he remembered how the British celebrated the end of hostilities by blowing up the main ammunition dumps as they left for home.

'Terrible bangs and flashes up, up into the sky. Such noise.'

Less than three years later, his family house and farm were taken during the First Arab–Israeli War in 1948. He and his family fled the fighting, going east to Jordan.

'Come,' he said one early evening. We walked up the street and across rough ground towards the edge of the village. I didn't know what we were doing, but Abu Joseph looked determined,

Archaeological excavation Caribbean style. The Silver Sands dig in Barbados, when I was just a newbie, was the most idyllic setting I have ever worked in.

Say 'Arrgh!' Male, old and dead for 800 years, my first skeleton was found underneath the ancient campsite on Silver Sands. Talk about a close-knit community!

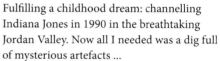

Fulfilling a childhood dream: channelling Indiana Jones in 1990 in the breathtaking Jordan Valley. Now all I needed was a dig full of mysterious artefacts ...

The Wadi Fidan dig, my first ever in Jordan. Stupidly hot, remote and in the middle of an international crisis, it was enough to drive you mad – if a colleague didn't beat you to it!

I returned to Jordan in 1991 for another dig, this time working through layers of powdered bat poop. The reward was great. Hidden beneath a false floor, the incredible Cave of the Bear site at Wadi al-Yabis offered a snapshot of Neolithic family life.

Our beige brick dig: the temple ruins at Tell es-Sweyhat in northern Syria. The Bronze Age site was fascinating, but the challenge of separating ordinary soil and decayed mud bricks haunted my dreams.

Dig accommodation in northern Syria was a house and a barrel to wash in. Spartan, but the collegiate old-school atmosphere more than compensated.

The Citadel of Aleppo, circa 1991. Sadly, this extraordinary pile of masonry – never captured by an invading force in antiquity – is under siege again. The damage may be irreparable.

The fabulously (and accurately) named 'Street Called Straight', a highlight of my downtime in Damascus.

My proudest moment as a consultant at Waltham Abbey in the UK: the unorthodox but successful raising of a 200-year-old wreck.

Outside the former Royal gunpowder mills at the Abbey: 72 hectares of significant archaeology (not to mention the explosives) and one young archaeologist without a clue. What could possibly go wrong?

These rusting barrel hoops on Dirk Hartog Island off the West Australian coast were evocative evidence of the *Persévérant*'s shipwrecked survivors on the island.

Looking for a message in a bottle buried 230 years ago. Those weeks at the Turtle Bay dig on Dirk Hartog Island felt like living on the edge of the earth.

Scurvy, the scourge of sea-faring dental work! Being marooned on a true desert island did no favours for the already ailing crew of the French whaler *Persévérant*.

Not quite a chain gang! A team excavates the tiny cells of C Division at Pentridge Prison, Melbourne. Declared unfit for human habitation in 1880, the cells were still in use well into the 1970s.

The infamous and miserable H Division, temporary home of Chopper Read.

This is the remains of one of three remarkable 'panopticon' exercise yards we uncovered at the site of the A Division cells in Pentridge. A revolutionary social experiment, the panopticon system ended up doing more harm than good.

'Everyone try to look natural.' Filming *Ned Kelly Uncovered* with Sir Tony Robinson during excavation of Ann Jones's Inn at Glenrowan, Victoria. (Photo Miriam Kenter)

A Martini-Henry rifle cartridge gave witness to the lethal gun battle that finished the Kelly gang and cemented the legend. (Photo Jon Sterenberg)

The smallest but most exciting find on the Glenrowan dig: a percussion cap last handled by Ned Kelly himself during the ferocious siege. (Photo Jon Sterenberg)

Working through a story point between takes of *Who's Been Sleeping in My House?* with director Darren Hutchinson. For those first few episodes of the show I had no idea what I was doing.

By series three, I was older and wiser, but still slightly nervous of the huge camera rig swinging above my head. Nice tracking shot, though!

From one skeleton to another: both younger and older than our man in Barbados, this 10,000-year-old child burial had to be excavated during a sandstorm in Boncuklu Höyük, Central Anatolia, Turkey.

and I'd noticed he had an old leather bag in his hand. We walked for ten minutes or so in silence, which was just as well, as I was having trouble keeping up with the wiry fellow.

When I caught up with him at last, he was standing looking out over the extraordinary rift valley towards the West Bank. The sun was about an hour from setting and sat low and deep orange over the Holy Land. As always, I was stunned by this view. Abu Joseph picked at the buckles of the leather satchel and pulled out an ancient pair of binoculars. Briefly, he held them to his eyes and adjusted the focus, then handed them to me.

'Look,' he pointed towards the far bank of the valley. 'You see? There, a white house with a wall?'

I scanned the valley edge where he was pointing and saw a large house with numerous outbuildings and a white painted wall that looked like it enclosed a large courtyard. There were olive groves and vineyards to the north and south and cascading into the valley.

'Yes, I see it.'

'That's mine,' he said simply. 'All of it, mine, and I haven't been allowed to return since 1948.'

I lowered the field glasses and looked at him. His normally smiling face looked fierce. He took the binoculars and carefully packed them back into the satchel and turned away.

We walked back again in silence.

For the first two years after fleeing their home, Abu Joseph and his family had lived in two army-style tents on the outskirts of Amman. Forty years on, he and his wife and children and grandchildren still lived in the UN-run refugee camp.

We were invited to his home. It sat in the heart of the enormous UN camp along a dusty narrow street. We were ushered through a decorated steel door into a small tiled courtyard surrounded by high grey concrete block walls. Abu Joseph's house was small, consisting of four rooms and a little kitchen. I remembered the beautiful sprawling house overlooking the Jordan Valley, his birthright. He had been a refugee for most of his adult life. His children and grandchildren had been refugees for their whole lives and they were just one of hundreds of thousands of Palestinian families living in exile in Jordan. My mind reeled from the complexity and difficulty of trying to find peace in the region when both sides have been so badly treated and the rage of injustice constantly simmers. I felt sorry for Abu Joseph, and I felt sorry for the Jewish Diaspora desperate to forge a new, safe life for their families. What a mess. What an ongoing tragedy.

*

Despite all the challenges that archaeologists face in remote places around the world, such as the climate and nasty wildlife, the greatest risk to life is travelling in vehicles, whether it's on dodgy coaches, overcrowded minibuses, or pants-wetting taxi trips where it's clear the driver has concluded that whether he lives or dies is up to God, and he's cool with that.

One day I almost became a statistic.

I'd been working on a Bronze Age settlement site in a busy little town at the northern end of the Jordan Valley called Shuna. I was driving a big old Nissan Patrol and accompanied by a laconic but funny Scot called George. I don't think he liked me on account that I was English. So when I said, 'George, I think we have a problem,' he gave a non-committal grunt. Maybe he thought I was trying to broach the North–South issue.

We were driving down a long, gently weaving road, which dropped quite steeply into the Jordan Valley, and I had just touched on the brakes as the Patrol started to gather speed.

The brake pedal hit the floor, offering no resistance at all.

As I pumped the brake with no effect, I said, in a slightly more shrill voice, 'No, George, we seriously have a problem. We've got no brakes.'

Ahead was an old pale-blue Datsun pick-up, which was trundling along, and I was catching it up very quickly. Unfortunately, there was a rusty old truck belching black smoke and grinding its way up the hill towards me, and I wasn't sure whether I was going to be able to overtake the Datsun without becoming a grille decoration for the truck.

Mercifully, George didn't say, 'Are you sure?' because I would have probably brought his head down onto the dashboard.

Instead, he said with grim resignation, 'Oh,' and braced against the dashboard himself.

I tried to drop down a gear, but we were going too fast. Even if the handbrake was actually attached to anything, which I doubted, I thought that it might send us off the road or into the path of the truck. Soon the Patrol was almost bouncing, and I pulled out from behind the pick-up and bore down on the menacing truck crawling towards us. Fortunately, the truck was really crawling, so I managed to swing back onto the right side of the road with about a metre to spare between the three of us.

The path was clear ahead, but both George and I knew that the roads in these parts were frequently used as a playground by school kids or were obstructed by goats or farm machinery. Any of which would have been a disaster with two tonnes of loose Japanese four-wheel-drive centre-lining it.

We were really flying now, and I could feel the steering getting light. Any sharp turn would result in our joining the depressing collections of burnt-out car wrecks on the sides of roads.

George looked over at me. 'I don't want to die at the hands of an Englishman, all right? So keep it steady.'

Luckily, it was a Friday, Jordan's one-day weekend, and the road ahead remained clear. Soon it started to flatten out and we approached the base of the valley. About five kilometres further on, I was able to use the gears to bring us to a stop.

It turned out that the mechanic had forgotten to put three of the brake pads back on when the car was serviced. After that, George and I were good mates.

*

The trouble with the Middle East is that despite all its faults and dangers, if you spend any amount of time there beyond a fleeting tourist visit, it gets under your skin. I have spoken to many who say, 'Oh yeah, it'll be in you forever,' in a tone like *everyone knows that*. Well, I wish someone had bloody told me, because I spent the next three years there. Even though I haven't been back for over twenty years, I think of it often with an almost homesick pang.

Only a few months after first vowing never to return, I found myself sitting at a noisy café in the centre of the town of Ajloun in the beautiful mountainous region of northern Jordan. I'd been invited to join a small team from Harvard. I'd like to say it was my internationally renowned intellect that got me the gig with such a prestigious college, but no. I had briefly met the project director, Ian, at a UN party in Amman about six months before. We'd had a good chat over a few beers that night and he'd asked me if I would be interested in joining his project. I'd said yes, not expecting for a moment that a drunken offer would be remembered. But I should have known. With a few notable exceptions (which I'll touch on later), the Americans I have worked with and others I have met on my travels have been some of the greatest people I have ever encountered. And Ian and the team gathered around the table in the café in Ajloun were some of the very best.

Much of the Middle East is desert or, if you are feeling charitable, a bit parched, and many people are bewildered that it could be described as the cradle of civilisation and the birthplace of agriculture.

Iraq ed-Dubb, or the Cave of the Bear, sits below a forested escarpment just to the north-west of Ajloun. Its large mouth is a dramatic scar in the craggy limestone cliff that overlooks the ordered pomegranate and pistachio orchards lying at the base of the Wadi al-Yabis. It's also one of the most significant early Neolithic archaeological sites in Jordan.

As I've mentioned, the most radical change in human history, the movement from hunter-gathering to farming, first began in the Middle East, and archaeological evidence discovered at Iraq ed-Dubb was some of the earliest. It showed the transition with the presence of both wild and domesticated wheat and barley grains, the emergence of new stone tools and simple but accomplished houses, and gave an intimate glimpse into the changes of that most personal task, the burial of one's nearest and dearest.

Combined with the adventurous and romantic location of the cave and the great team, the project was one of the best I have worked on. But it might not have happened at all if it hadn't been for a moment of uncharacteristic frustration by my good friend Louise Martin.

The cave had been used by goats and bats as a shelter for eons, and so the first couple of days were spent unpleasantly excavating a knee-deep layer of powdered poop. I'm sure in Australia or the

UK, we would have had to put on Hazmat suits and respirators, but there we just dealt with it with bandanas across our faces.

It was a large cave, ten metres high and wide by about fifteen metres deep. So there was a lot of poop to move, but we got it done. The problem was we found nothing underneath except the rocky base of the cave. We sat dejected, filthy as coal miners, with the grime of a thousand years of bat crap sunk into our pores. There was no archaeology. Ian, the director, couldn't believe it. The location of the cave and artefacts discovered at its mouth during a previous survey strongly suggested that the cave had been occupied in antiquity. I sat there and started to think about what I was going to do for the next three months. Then Louise stood up, picked up a mattock and hefted it over her shoulder.

'Bloody bugger,' she said and swung the mattock with frustration down onto the rocky ground.

But instead of bouncing off the rock, it disappeared partially below the surface. We all looked at the mattock now standing by itself, half-buried in the floor of the cave, next to a very surprised Louise. Immediately, I thought that the mattock had broken. Then for a fleeting moment, I thought that Lou was superhuman. Finally, I came to the same conclusion as everyone else.

This wasn't the rocky base of the cave. It was a thin calcareous crust that must have built up over the years, sealing the soil deposits below. We crowded around and saw that the crust was only a couple of centimetres thick, and with a renewed enthusiasm we set to and started smashing our way into the past.

Over the next couple of months, we discovered an intimate scene, a snapshot of the lives of a family group that had made the cave their home ten thousand years ago. Two small oval hut structures were discovered with remarkably well-preserved stone walls that stood to thigh height in parts. About five metres across, they were carefully lined with plaster, and there was evidence that a small fire had been set in the middle of one of the huts and a grinding stone into the plaster floor of the other. While the cave afforded some protection from the elements, the mouth was large enough, and the winters in this part of Jordan sufficiently cold, for the construction of huts to be a good idea. Thousands of stone artefacts and tiny remains of plants and animals showed that the occupants of the Cave of the Bear had lived in that Pre-Pottery Neolithic crossover period between hunter-gathering and farming. It seemed that they still sought food from the wild but had also started to grow early forms of domesticated barley. It was an incredibly well-preserved site, and even more remarkably, we encountered some of the original occupants.

In a fashion similar to the burials in Barbados, we found two skeletons, an adolescent and adult male, buried under the floors of the huts. Due to the real cave floor being just below the floors of the huts, the bodies of our family's nearest and dearest would have been close to the action. Gag-makingly close.

Looking out at the beautiful Wadi al-Yabis framed by the ragged mouth of the cave, I wondered whether the landscape was the same then. Did our family sit around the fire and take in the same view? I guess not much would have changed, apart from a few dry stone walls outlining tiny fields and the pistachio and pomegranate orchards that now lay at the base of the valley.

Their histories are always going to be fragmentary at this great antiquity, but these people weren't that different from us. I imagine they wanted to feel safe, not too hungry and have a roof over their heads, and maybe enjoy a bit of a laugh and a singsong around the fire.

*

The archaeologist's job is to grub around in the dirt, leaving no rock unturned in the pursuit of knowledge of our past. So in places like the Middle East, we are often confronted by horrible things that live in dark and cool spaces. And the most horrible and frankly terrifying thing I have ever encountered is without a doubt the camel spider. I am sure that somewhere there is a weirdo who thinks they are 'cute' and 'interesting', but so far I haven't met anyone who has encountered these desert monsters and doesn't shudder at the memory. They are the stuff of nightmares, and twenty years down the track, they still occasionally haunt mine.

I first saw a camel spider in the moonlight. Sitting around a camp fire, I saw this thing skitter across the desert floor. It was moving at speed and I mistook it for a rat at first. But it stopped, reared up onto its hind legs and waggled these huge front legs into the air before haring off again. I sounded the alarm and we all cautiously pursued it, each of us trying valiantly to be at the back of the group.

Briefly, the moon went behind a small cloud, and then we were bathed in bright silver light and the camel spider was standing still in front of us. We could clearly see that it was huge, easily as big as a large outstretched hand. It was pale and hairless with large legs and an abdomen like an elongated hen's egg. At the front were two huge pincers that were constantly moving, as were its two front legs, which did not seem to be used for support or to run, but instead were forever reaching and grasping at the air in front of it, trying to pull anything into its nasty jaws. We stopped in a comic huddle. The moon was behind us and our shadows almost reached the beast. It turned towards us. Normally, animals bugger off when humans approach. 'Go slowly so you don't frighten it away', or in the case of snakes, 'Make a load of noise and you'll be fine'. And the old chestnut, 'They're more afraid of you than you are of them'. Well none of these wise bits of advice apply to camel spiders.

For a second we looked at it and it looked at us, creepily beckoning with its front legs. And then it charged at us. Squealing, we turned and fled. Camel spiders can run at sixteen kilometres an hour, which is a terrifying pace when people are getting in your way, in the dark, in the middle of the desert. It stayed with us for about a hundred metres before stopping and trotting off in its original direction, satisfied that it had completely freaked us out.

The Jordanian guys who worked on the digs hated them and would batter them to pieces with their shovels whenever one was uncovered. They are not actually spiders but are part of the arachnid family and are closer to scorpions (so that's much better). The story goes that they are called camel spiders because they use their powerful jaws to snip through the tough hide of camels and drink their blood. I've not read anything to confirm this but can certainly believe it.

They menaced me for years, either directly – I would hear them scuttling around the dig house at night, or they would jump out of a burrow or from under a rock when I was working and then chase after me like the schoolyard bully – or indirectly through numerous stories of horrible encounters told by other archaeologists over beers in the safety of a hotel lobby bar.

I heard that the reason they run towards you is to get into your shadow and not to strip your flesh from the bone. But I don't believe it. There is nothing benign about them. One time, with trousers firmly embraced by the tops of my army boots, I stood my ground, and one of the buggers attacked my foot for about twenty minutes, snip-snip-snipping at the tough boot leather, making little gouges. I'm sure it would have continued until it had whittled a hole through the boot if it hadn't been dispatched with excessive force by one of the Arab workers.

*

Raiders of the Lost Ark is Steven Spielberg's action film about a Harvard archaeologist's battle against the forces of evil and his quest to discover the greatest biblical treasure, the Ark of the Covenant. It was released when I was eleven and reinforced my determination to be an archaeologist. If you meet an archaeologist born after about 1970 who claims that Indiana Jones had no hand in their career choice, they're lying. The movie also piqued my interest in adventure. It wasn't till later that I discovered that the adventures of Indiana Jones, or his real-life counterparts such as Freya Stark and Wilfred Thesiger, belonged to an era that was gone, if only recently so. I remember feeling sad about this and disappointed that I had not been born in the late nineteenth century, into a world where there were still places to discover.

Then one glorious evening, accompanied by some of my team mates from the Iraq ed-Dubb project, I walked down the narrow ravine called the Siiq and into an adventure. Described as the 'rose-red city half as old as time', Petra is the extraordinary Nabatean city that lay hidden and forgotten in the folds of the Jebel al-Madhbah mountains in southern Jordan for over a thousand years. I say I walked into an adventure because, despite the tourists and the hawkers selling gaudy gifts, Petra is so extraordinary, so otherworldly it felt like I had stumbled into the pages of *The Lost World* or *King Solomon's Mines*.

With special permits from the Department of Antiquities to camp out in Petra, we headed into the sandstone valleys that branch off in every direction and shaped the way this unique settlement formed. Petra has always been known by the Bedouin of the region, but it wasn't until 1812 that it was rediscovered by the western world, and the archaeological ruins, in their impossibly romantic location, became a fascination for Victorian antiquarians and archaeologists.

The entrance to Petra lies on the outskirts of the town of Wadi Musa, or Moses Spring, in a deep ravine. Wadi Musa is where Moses struck his staff on a rock and water issued forth, saving his people yet again. Amazingly, there is a rock where water bubbles out of the top. Less biblically, it now cascades into a dirty little concrete trough. A small, basic building was thrown over the site, and when I was there, the insides of this holy spot were crudely graffitied with love hearts and the odd cock and balls.

The rock forming the vertical walls of the Siiq is richly coloured in swirls of reds and oranges and purples, even greens. The narrow ravine runs for almost a kilometre through the mountains. We made our echoing way down and stopped, gasping in wonder, at the image that opened up before us at the end. Carved into the cliff opposite the Siiq is the most recognisable feature of Petra, the Al Khazneh or the Treasury. It's actually a tomb with a beautifully ornate façade carved out of the rock. Its sheltered position means that it's the best preserved of the large rock-cut façades that are found throughout the valleys of Petra. The Treasury features in the movie *Indiana Jones and the Last Crusade*, in which it is depicted as the final resting place of the Holy Grail, the cup used by Christ at the Last Supper. The movie shows a huge cavern behind the façade where Dr Jones has to overcome fiendishly complex tests before confronting a 700-year-old knight and choosing the right cup from a twinkling array of ornate chalices. Fortunately, the movie was released after I had been to Petra, otherwise I would have been devastated to discover that beyond the entrance to the Treasury is only a small plain room, a burial chamber, smelling faintly of wee. The Treasury is an elaborate façade to a tomb constructed in the classical Greek tradition in the first century AD.

Going past the Treasury down the main valley, other tombs and temples are evidence that this dry, remote and frankly inhospitable spot was once a glorious, thriving and beautiful city. Petra was founded by the Edomites around the third century BC but achieved its stunning pinnacle under the Nabateans, who over the next three hundred years developed Petra as the main administrative and trading centre of their large territory of the southern Levant. Anything successful naturally attracts unwanted attention, and Petra was taken forcefully by the Romans in 106 AD, during the rapid expansion of the empire into the Middle East, in the reign of Emperor Trajan.

I visited Petra many times but a couple of instances stand out. The funniest was a funeral held there in 1992 (no, really).

Mike was a brilliant character and archaeologist on the Jordan scene and had spent many years exploring Petra. He was fit as a fiddle and always up for a laugh, and I had much fun in his company in the short time I knew him. When I met him he was working with the local Petra Bedouin, the Bidul, studying how they lived within the ruins, and he had built up a great friendship with the community.

It was during one of these ethnographic surveys, and while I was on my last project in Jordan, that Mike suddenly died. He'd been bitten by a tick and suffered a catastrophic reaction to Mediterranean tick fever. The archaeological community in Jordan is small and tight-knit, and his death shocked and saddened us. But his funeral was hilarious.

As testament to the relationship that Mike had built up with the Bidul, they honoured him by donating a plot of land for his burial overlooking Petra and opposite the Byzantine Church where he had excavated for years. The funeral was a grand affair with tents erected and all the Bedouin elders present. Many archaeologists from all over the world were also present. By and large, archaeologists are an amiable and harmless bunch. Perhaps we are a little more OCD than other groups, and maybe there are a few eccentrics, but no more than any other academic bunch. But at that time a fully paid-up nut was directing archaeological excavations at another site in Petra.

He was American, from Texas, I think, and he ran his projects like a military operation. His poor students and other diggers were billeted in tents in the valley next to the sites, and they were forbidden to leave Petra, even to head into nearby Wadi Musa for a kebab. They were required to wear military-style work clothes, and seniority was identified by coloured tabs on their epaulettes (nothing for diggers, blue for trench leaders, green for supervisors …). It was rumoured that a red tab marked an unfortunate female student as his 'favourite'. He was in his fifties and he rode around Petra, also in military fatigues, on the back of a white horse, carrying two pearl-handled pistols in cowboy holsters at his waist. He was clearly unconventional but had managed to raise funding for his dig year after year. I'm sure the Bedouin thought he was an oddball, but he left them alone, and so they shrugged and gave him a wide berth.

Unfortunately, he took it upon himself to oversee the funeral ceremony.

The first shock of the day came when Mike's two wives and recent fiancée met for the first time. When they realised who each of them were, there was a stunned silence, and all the archaeologists stared down at their teacups and shuffled away. We could hardly look at each other but we could sense others struggling not to laugh, shoulders shaking and puce faces pretending to look at tombs or examine a shard of pottery that had been hastily scooped up. Mike was from Utah, but no one had any inkling that he had been Mormon. And even if he was, the practice of polygamy is very rare and not nowadays considered part of the mainstream faith. Again, it was a measure of the respect that was had for the man that his newly acquainted partners didn't make a scene but simply stood apart from each other for the rest of the day.

The morning was passing and the valley was getting oppressively hot, but there was no sign of our gun-toting host. It was not only inconvenient but also exceptionally rude to keep the Bedouin leaders waiting, and most of us were wanting to get into the cold beer at the wake.

Another hour passed. The elders were looking scandalised and everyone else was fidgeting when, in the distance, appeared our man, clad astonishingly in white Arab formal dress, like Peter O'Toole in *Lawrence of Arabia*, right down to the curved dagger at his belt ... and he was riding a camel. Everyone looked agog at the sight of him swaying and lurching his way towards us. For the second time that day, I could see people having trouble holding it together. One of the Bedouin leaders shook his head and covered his eyes.

Eventually, our host made it up the short slope to where we stood. He paused and, with a flourish, flicked back his snow-white cape and gave us a manic smile. He opened his mouth, no doubt to make some grand statement, but the camel decided at that moment to die. The poor animal let out an enormous bellow and lurched forwards, hitting the ground with a terrible thump and throwing 'Lawrence' sprawling into the dust. It let out one last sigh, twitched a leg and was still.

There was a moment of stunned silence as the whole group processed what had just happened. It was the straw that broke the camel's back (so to speak), and everyone fell about laughing.

Our host was struggling to untangle himself from the bridle and his voluminous cape but we were incapable of helping. Tears streamed down people's faces; we were doubled over in hysterics, leaning on each other's shoulders, shaking with laughter, and it was a long time before any of us could pull it together and get on with the ceremony. Once he had untangled himself, our intrepid host, red in the face with anger and embarrassment, stomped off and wasn't seen again either on that day or days after. He never dug at Petra again.

Mike would have loved it all.

*

Most projects that I worked on in Jordan had site guards. I've never been sure why. Even a casual glance from the uninitiated would show that none of the sites had the remotest potential to yield anything worth any money (the curse of digging early prehistoric sites when chipped stone and dirt is all that is found), but more puzzling were the guards themselves.

They were always extraordinarily old and frail. One notable protector of our archaeological treasures was blind. In the mornings he would greet me enthusiastically, claiming that peace would be upon me, while looking three feet to the right of my ear with his milky white eyes. Worryingly, he was never without an ancient rifle. The age of candidates for this role was the result of the perceived honour of such a position, so naturally it was given to the most senior member of the community. Most of the time the position seemed ceremonial at best, but occasionally these old guys were life-savers …

This one day in Petra, I was completely lost. I'd gone through the various phases: not knowing where I was; annoyance but quiet confidence that I'd get back on the right track if I kept going; progressing to a slight flutter of anxiety – it's really hot, I only have half a bottle of water – at which point I bluffed, shook my head, spoke out loud about what an idiot I was and how I'd have a bloody good laugh about it later; and galloping on to cold fear, with the crashing realisation that I was completely lost and had been for a couple of hours.

So that's where I was as I stood, back against the canyon wall in a tiny slither of shade. In a cavalier mood, I had struck off from the main tourist track and wandered through the twisting, narrow gorges that radiated in all directions. Each turn surprised me with a row of rock-cut homes or more modest tombs. The sunny blue sky was a thin ribbon above, and very soon I was completely disorientated. It was somewhere in the maze of little-mapped and less-visited canyons and gullies branching off the main spectacular valley of Petra that I had a little panic.

Even here, miles away from the famous tombs, rock-cut caves showed the broad extent of the ancient city. It was just a pity everyone who knew the way back had been dead for a thousand years or more.

I'd gone off for a weekend by myself, so I wouldn't be missed for another two days. By that time I'd be a piece of biltong.

Then a voice, which sounded like it was coming from near my right ankle, croaked, 'Hello, sir,' in heavily accented English.

'Jesus Christ!' I said as I leaped about ten feet into the air.

With my heart beating in my throat, I looked at a raggedy old man lying at the base of the canyon cliff, half-jammed under an overhang that was knee-high from the ground. He was wrapped in a dusty old robe and looked about two hundred years old. The red henna staining his short grey beard identified him as a hajji – a pilgrim who had made the Hajj to Mecca – and I treated him formally and with as much respect as I could muster considering the fright he had given me. Actually, my fright soon changed to concern, because he looked like he was on his last legs, or in this case his last side, but he waved me over with a wizened hand.

I sat in the sand in front of him and exchanged some more formal greetings. I had learned that a conversation in Jordan made up entirely of greetings could go on for ten minutes or more. If strung together with inquiries about one's health, it could stretch out to twice as long.

'Hello.'

'Peace be with you.'

'And with you too.'

'Hello.'

'Hello.'

(... pause ...)

'Peace be with you.'

'And with you too.'

'Hello.'

'How are you?'

'Very well, thanks be to God, and with you?'

'Well, thanks be to God ...'

'Hello.'

After a while he stopped, apparently satisfied that I was well greeted and well in myself.

He looked off down the sandy floor of the canyon and my eyes followed. We were in the middle of bloody nowhere. What was he doing here? I couldn't see or hear any goats, so he wasn't a goatherd. He coughed then cackled like an old person in the movies and asked me what I did. His English was limited to the first 'Hello, sir' and my Arabic has never been very good, but I understood these basic questions and knew how to say, 'I'm an archaeologist.'

He cackled again (not an uncommon response, I'm afraid) and started rummaging in the folds of his robe, talking rapidly. I could only catch the word 'archaeologist'.

He brought out a large leather wallet and from it gently drew out a folded piece of paper. Brown, stained and frayed thin at the folds, it looked as old as him.

I suddenly thought, *Oh my God, it's a map. With his last gasping, cackling breath in this lonely spot he's going to give me the map to a wondrous archaeological treasure.*

I was so excited. Of course, I would have been saddened by his noble passing and would pause to close his eyes, but then I would be rich or famous or, ideally, both!

With trembling hands, I accepted the proffered document. And with the Indiana Jones movie theme playing in my head, I gingerly opened it up. I frowned. It wasn't a map. It was a letter, written on a typewriter and dated 1956.

It was addressed 'To Whom It May Concern', and stated that the holder of this letter – I glanced up at the wrinkled old roll of cloth in front of me, who now seemed to be trying to glow with pride and was doing surprisingly well – was employed as a guard on an archaeological site and was thoroughly trustworthy, and the author would not hesitate to recommend him for similar roles on other projects. It was signed 'Diana Kirkbride'. I was staggered, firstly, that he would keep such a thing for over thirty years and, secondly, that he had worked for the famous Diana Kirkbride. Diana was an alumnus of my university, a pioneer of Near Eastern Archaeology and supposedly a prodigious gin drinker. She had learned to dig under the tutelage of Sir Max Mallowan, husband of Agatha Christie, and had got the taste for gin undoubtedly from working with Dame Kathleen Kenyon at Jericho.

The former guard was pleased at my surprise, and I congratulated him and told him that I knew of Diana. I tried to let him know that she was still alive, although retired. I don't think he got any of what I said, except Diana, but he was so pleased that we shook hands for a long time. It was a strangely moving moment and I remember it very clearly: the pride of a man held in a simple letter. I have often wondered what Diana Kirkbride would have thought had she known the effect her kind words had had on his life.

Before I left I asked him how I could get to Wadi Musa. He pointed down the canyon and nodded. Half an hour later I was hailing a beaten-up Datsun truck on a road that I recognised as the route to the Bedouin village to the north of Petra.

I was tired, hot and very thirsty, and the only room was in the back of the pick-up, which was already crowded with four large goats and two grim-looking old women. I hopped in, smiled briefly at the nearest woman and huddled down with a goat's arse in my face. The goats stank and one of them farted about every thirty seconds. But no matter, the day was nearly over, I was safe and headed towards the hotel and a nice cold beer. I could handle this short half-hour trip. Then one of the old women passed me what looked like a white and dusty cue ball. I groaned. Luckily, the sound was covered by the nearest goat breaking wind into my ear. I'd heard about this Bedouin delicacy and it didn't sound good. The cue ball was made from desiccated goat's yoghurt, and it was a favourite of goatherds, who could be seen chewing on it as they wandered after their flocks.

I tried to refuse, but she gave me such a scowl and vigorous nod that I started gnawing on it with feigned enthusiasm. My eyes watered as I nodded and mumbled, 'Good, very good,' at her. It was terrible. Imagine biting down on a hard lump of mouth-drying sour chalk. Now imagine kissing a hot goat's bottom. Got that? It was worse.

OF SECRET ARCHIVES, A CHOMPING TREE AND ELEPHANT-HIDE TILES

... there were rumours of Martians ... and news of the destruction of Waltham Abbey Powder Mills in a vain attempt to blow up one of the invaders.

HG Wells, *The War of the Worlds*, 1898

It was while Christmas shopping after returning from the Middle East for the last time that I started to feel unwell, but I wasn't going to let a cold spoil my fun. Christmas shopping is one of those 'love it or hate it' activities, but I bloody love it. I am happily and proudly a sentimental fool and indulge and revel in the whole Christmas thing. From getting an advent calendar and advent candle to risking the exasperation of my wife, Inga, by purchasing yet another armful of tinsel and decorations, I have always plunged headfirst into the sherry-filled swimming pool that is the celebration of the birth of a person I'm not sure existed but who has the best birthday ever, every year.

Anyway, I was weaving my way along Kensington High Street after a successfully bustling shopping day. It was dark but dry and cold and I had that slightly squiffy warm feeling following an afternoon of 'bank crawling'. It seems mad now, but back then the high street banks celebrated Christmas by inviting their customers in for free cups of mulled wine and mince pies. I suppose these were intended for customers of those particular banks, but I, like a number of others, hopped in and out of the cold crowds, pretending to look at mortgage brochures while sucking back the spicy wine. Then we employed a variety of mimes to justify an exit without actually doing any banking. Mine was to finish my drink, look at the wall clock in horror, then at my watch and rush out the door in a pantomime of panic, muttering lamentations about being late. The staff working the front doors – Santa hats and bauble earrings – handing out the pies and steaming cups of wine must have found it hilarious but gracefully never let on that we all looked like a herd of time-conscious meerkats with wine-stained teeth.

I started to feel a bit shivery and the telltale sandpaper throat told me that I had only a couple of hours before the ubiquitous tonsillitis throttled me into a miserable heap.

This was not good. Not at any time but particularly now. All my Middle East days had been voluntary. Now I was due to start a new job, a proper, grown-up paying job, in two days' time. I didn't have a doctor or, as I have mentioned before, a clue, so getting antibiotics wasn't on the cards. I was sleeping on a friend's sofa in a draughty dump in North London, and I had to get up to my sister's the next day because the job was in Newcastle-under-Lyme in Staffordshire, about 300 kilometres to the northwest of the capital.

Bugger that, I thought, *it's Christmas; I will not get tonsillitis,* and so I pushed through and went to the pub for farewell drinks with friends.

The next day or so was a haze of hangover and fever. On the morning I was to start work, my sister, Debbie, hauled me to the doctor, who pulled a face when she looked down my throat, stuck what felt like a red-hot knitting needle into my left bum cheek and gave me a course of penicillin.

If it hadn't been the first day at a new job, I would have crawled back to bed. My throat was so sore I could hardly speak, I had a roaring temperature and I was quite delirious. But Deb had teed up this job for me, and so off I staggered into the offices of the Royal Commission on the Historical Monuments of England at the Keele University Campus, just north of Newcastle-under-Lyme in Staffordshire.

The royal commission was established by royal warrant to discover, assess and record buildings and monuments of historical importance across the country. Other commissions were established at the same time to record monuments in Scotland and Wales. The royal commission is now part of English Heritage.

The first day would have been farcical if I hadn't been feeling so terrible. It was a small office of about ten or so archaeologists and historians, who were kind enough to come up and meet me when I arrived. Their smiles became ever so fixed when confronted with the sweaty young man who croaked an unintelligible greeting. The office was stuffy and I was going downhill quite rapidly, but I tried to focus. I was taken to a meeting room and Wayne Cocroft, one of the senior commission officers, started to fill me in on the organisation, the project that I was to help with and what my immediate tasks would be. Wayne was a great fellow and one of Deb's old friends, so I was trying my best to rally and pay attention. But to no avail.

Midway through this induction, I passed out, suddenly pitching forward, and smacked my face hard on the table in front of Wayne. This brought me round again, and jerking back upright, I continued to listen as if nothing had happened. Wayne, as only an Englishman would do in such a situation, chose to ignore the fact that I had just headbutted the table and doggedly continued to explain the job. Later, he admitted that he had thought this was a little strange and perhaps a commentary on the dullness of his delivery.

As luck would have it, I had started on the day of the office Christmas drinks, so from lunch until I judged I could leave without being rude, I stood, *stood*, for four hours, croaking small talk to my new colleagues in an overheated and packed pub. But the antibiotics kicked in, and I started to feel much better over the next couple of days. Of course, I then stopped taking the rest of the course of penicillin.

The job was great, but before I could get stuck into it, we broke up for the Christmas holidays. I bade everyone a merry Christmas and, later than I'd hoped, started the long drive over the border and through Wales to my parents' little cottage, nestled in a wooded valley in Pembrokeshire. It was already getting dark as I drove out of Stoke towards the medieval town of Shrewsbury. Within a couple of miles I hit the thickest fog I have ever witnessed. Visibility dropped to a matter of feet. I couldn't see the far side of the road. I couldn't see the near side of the road. Everyone was driving at a crawl, many with their hazard lights on. I soon lost track of where I was, but I wasn't overly concerned until I started to feel unwell again. In the back of my mind I remembered my mother, who was a nurse, mentioning that not finishing a course of antibiotics was a bad thing.

The thick blanket of fog covered the whole of Wales, and a journey that should have taken five hours took nine. By the time I reached the little old cottage, I was desperately unwell and collapsed into bed with uncontrollable shakes, unable to tell my worried mum what was going on.

By lunch the following day I was saying 'aah' into the face of a concerned-looking doctor, who told my parents to go straight to the hospital in Carmarthen, forty-five minutes away, and that she would make sure someone was waiting for us.

Nothing says 'You're really not very well' more clearly than being met at the Accident and Emergency entrance by a doctor, two nurses and a wheelchair. This unusual reception was not lost on my mother, who had worked for years in the National Health System, so the last thing I saw as I was whisked away was a very worried-looking parent. I was confused. I had tonsillitis. Sure, it was very unpleasant but not worth all this fuss. I was transferred to a large padded chair in a treatment room. A giant of a doctor came in wearing shirtsleeves and braces and had a look down my throat. By then I was finding it difficult to breathe. He glanced at the two nurses that were standing on either side of the chair. Then he calmly told me that I had a serious throat infection, an abscess behind my left tonsil called a 'quinsy', which was obstructing my airway. He would have to cut into it and drain the pus before things 'got out of hand'. I must have given him a WTF expression, because he apologised and said that it was going to really hurt.

I looked around at the nurses for a sign that he was joking, but they were moving into place. By linking their arms together and leaning with their whole body weight across my lap, they pinioned my arms and legs to the chair and, as disbelief freefell into panic, the doctor held open my mouth and sliced at the back of my raw and swollen throat with a scalpel.

This was over twenty-three years ago and I can still feel the pulling, slicing and tearing as he tried to cut my head off from the inside. It may seem that I am prone to fainting, but I think no more than the average person – in fact, I don't think I have fainted since – but I passed out twice in that chair. Each time, I came to and found myself still pinned down by two nurses ...

oh, how reality mocks my dreams ... and the doctor still merrily chopping away.

An hour and a half later (with a few breaks so the nurses could get the blood circulating in their arms), the doctor was satisfied that he had got all the pus out, and I slumped back in the chair, soaked to the skin with sweat.

'And that's how you treat a quinsy, is it?' I croaked.

He smiled. 'Yep, I'm afraid so.'

'In which century would that be, then?'

I spent Christmas and the following week in a hospital bed, feeling very sorry for myself, and have lived in fear of getting tonsillitis ever again.

I returned to the royal commission remarkably well, however, and embarked on a new phase of my archaeological career. The project was the survey and recording of a former explosives factory north of London, on the edge of the medieval market town of Waltham Abbey in Essex.

*

In 1991 an extraordinary thing happened. A war that never was, ended. Essentially, the Cold War was a 44-year playground strop between two bullies who menaced each other and everyone else with big sticks. Looking back, it's pathetic. The actions of the superpowers of the Soviet Union and United States during the Cold War would be risible if they hadn't caused so much misery and anxiety around the world. If my mother had been the UN president at the time, she would have given them both such a slap round the back of the legs.

The end of the Cold War led to a sharp demilitarisation, and the British Ministry of Defence started scything back some of its facilities and real estate. Waltham Abbey was closed, bringing the curtain down on a 300-year history of inventing and making things to kill people.

Up to this point, my research experience had consisted of hours at a photocopier duplicating scores of chapters and articles from archaeological texts, to be dutifully stapled and filed with very little chance that they would ever be read. We all did this at university. It made us feel good, as if we had achieved something. I would flop down next to my fellow archaeology students in the near empty student union bar (we were always the first ones in – well, apart from the sociology students, who seemed to actually live in the bar), exhausted but guilt-free after a long day in the library, copying everything in sight.

But as the years went on, we ended up reading some of what we copied and started to realise a couple of startling things: writing essays was made much easier and less stressful if one actually read about the subject, and conducting structured research was enjoyable. Nevertheless, by the time I left university, my research skills were still pretty rudimentary.

My main task at the royal commission was to research and record the history of the Waltham Abbey explosives site. Initially,

I sat there blinking and waiting for Wayne to give me detailed instructions on how to do this, the spoon-feeding that I was used to as a student. Where was the reading list, guidance on where to get the information, how many words he wanted? But he just sat and blinked back at me.

'Right,' I said. 'I'll get on with it then.'

Unguided research is an adventure of sorts, and discovering the history of Waltham Abbey was a challenge because much of the archive material was secret. It had been a government-run explosives factory and research facility, after all. So even though I discovered that a lot of the primary archive material was at the Public Records Office (PRO) in London, it wasn't publicly accessible. The PRO has two tasks: to store and catalogue records generated by government and public organisations, and to make records, deemed suitable, available to the public. Records available to the public are held at, or can be ordered from, the PRO at Kew, south-west of London. Records that either haven't been reviewed or are classified 'secret' are held at an old aerodrome in Hertfordshire. And it was here that the majority of the Waltham Abbey's archives were stored.

I was issued with one of the early portable computers (you could hardly call them laptops – perhaps you could perch it across two laps – a 'lapstop'?). The Amstrad PPC 512 was a big grey rectangle with a moulded handle at one end that flipped open to reveal a keyboard and a tiny liquid-crystal display. It was state of the art at the time and had about as much processing power as the average TV remote control these days. I was also given a train ticket to London and instructed to report to the site manager of the PRO repository in Hertfordshire.

On the Monday morning I got off the train and, after a quick look at the sketched map directions, walked off into the suburban streets. There were no way-signs or other indication that a major facility was in the area, and just when I was about to give up and backtrack, I saw a small faded sign at the end of a cul de sac of uniform postwar semi-detached houses, which informed me that I had arrived. I learned subsequently that despite what Cubby Broccoli and the Bond movies would have you believe, secret establishments are often disappointingly mundane, slightly rundown, almost invisible. Which, of course, is the idea.

There was a building only a short walk from the Institute of Archaeology in London that used to be the headquarters of the British Security Service, also known as MI5, the UK's domestic intelligence service. Its location was common knowledge amongst us neo-Trotskyite students, and we would rebelliously flick the Vs at the nest of security cameras at its entrance. But to most passers-by, it was a dull, unremarkable office building with about ten storeys of dirty windows obscured by rumpled net curtains. How very British to use net curtains to thwart lip-reading communist spies. But it blended in, not warranting a second, or even a first, look from the many office workers and commuters that hurried past. Don't bother looking for it now. MI5 moved out years ago and the drab building was pulled down.

The **PRO** archive that lay in front of me that day was the same. Hidden in plain sight was a group of wartime hangers and low, ugly red-brick buildings that housed some of the most sensitive secret material in the country.

A guard at the entrance radioed for an escort when I explained who I was, and I was taken by another sober-faced, middle-aged guard about forty metres to a double-storeyed block that served as the administration building for the site. After a short wait, I was shown into the manager's dull and unadorned room. If John le Carré was to describe a career intelligence civil servant's office, it would look like this. The manager was studying a slim file as I entered, then looked up, smiled and pointed to a chair.

I suppose I seemed very young and probably scruffy to the neat man of perhaps sixty who faced me across his almost empty desk. He immediately made it clear that this was an interrogation rather than a welcoming chat and made no secret of the fact that the file before him was about me. He lifted it up, briefly referred to the front page, and said, 'You're an archaeologist.'

'Yes.'

'And you're working for the Royal Commission on the Historical Monuments of England?'

'Yes.'

'And you are researching a Ministry of Defence facility at Waltham Abbey?'

'Yes.'

'Why?'

I hadn't anticipated this, and truth be told, I hadn't asked that question myself.

'I'm not entirely sure. I suppose it's historic,' I added lamely.

'And a monument, no doubt,' he added with smile. 'The documents you will be looking at are restricted. Permission for you to look at them has been given by the Ministry of Defence. However, you will be bound by the obligations of the Official Secrets Act. Sign here to show you understand and agree to comply.'

As I signed, I asked what the obligations were.

He handed me a copy of the 1989 Act and said, 'To keep secrets secret.'

My contract with the royal commission was initially for three months, so I asked how long I was obliged to comply with the Act.

He looked startled at such a silly question. 'Forever.'

He closed the file and said, while tap-tapping the beige cardboard front, 'I'm obliged to let you know that we are conducting background checks on you. Is there anything that you think I should know that may have a bearing on our opinion of your national security risk?'

Over the years I have wondered whether he was playing around with me, but he really didn't seem to be the prankster type. At that moment on a grey January morning in a dull little office in a nondescript building in the middle of an unremarkable housing estate under the Heathrow flight path, I thought of all the naughty things I had done: underage drinking and sly smokes; a number of 'student activities' that either involved marching and shouting or giggling and falling asleep; and of course forgetting to spy while I was in Syria.

It was disconcerting, not least because I realised I wasn't nearly the rebel I thought I was. 'No,' I said.

After that he lightened up and told me that scrutinisers worked here, reading millions of documents and deciding whether they were suitable for release to the public now or in ten, twenty-five, fifty or seventy-five years' time.

When I suggested that it was only a matter of time, then, before all our secrets would be known, he shook his head and pointed behind him out of the window to a row of tall, thin chimney stacks. 'I have six incinerators here because there are some secrets that are judged to never be in the public interest to release.'

While I shouldn't have been surprised, I was – and a little depressed by this.

I was told that I would be working in building B, that I was not to leave without an escort and I should restrict myself to the Waltham Abbey records.

Building B was a low concrete-roofed, blocky building with a few windows set high on the walls, so once inside there were no views except for glimpses of the grey clouds. It was unheated and completely empty, apart from plan chests and filing cabinets housing the documents that I was to pore over for the next six weeks. Two small rooms contained the files. In one was a large companion desk where I worked, and down the hall was a toilet. On the other side of the hall to the Waltham Abbey rooms were two timber doors. One said *Metropolitan Police* etched on a black label, the other just bore a number 2. With the warnings from the manager still fresh, I ignored the doors, but over the weeks my curiosity grew. I wasn't so interested in what was behind the Metropolitan Police door. It was wanting to know what lay behind the enigmatic number 2 door.

But I buckled down and got on with trying to make sense out of the hundreds of documents, maps and plans that made up the Waltham Abbey archive.

Waltham Abbey, like the other explosives factories across Britain and elsewhere, was an unusual factory in that the buildings were kept separate from each other, often by high earth mounds and considerable distances, to stop the whole factory going up in smoke if one building blew. So they are remarkably green and pleasant landscapes, considering their deadly products.

Waltham Abbey was particularly incongruous. It had been in the business of designing and making materials to kill people for a very long time. Lying on the banks of the River Lea, it had a canal system that linked various processing buildings, and these waterways, as well as a narrow gauge railway, wended their way between blast banks and through fields and woods. Buildings of a multitude of shapes, sizes and material stood either ruinous and moss covered or as if the workers had just left for lunch.

Being a government establishment, the different layouts of the site over time and details of each structure, down to the design of a window catch, were recorded in extraordinary detail and with amazing skill. Some of the early plans for the site and architectural drawings were works of art. Plans dated back to the late eighteenth century and up to the year of the site's closure in 1991. By cross-referencing the appearance of buildings and landscape features such as the rail and canal systems with other records, I was able to build a comprehensive picture of the development of the site, the function of all the buildings and the change in usage over time.

There's a great story that the Waltham Abbey explosives production started in the early sixteenth century with the abbey monks making gunpowder and flogging it to the government. Sadly, there is no evidence for this, although the land on which the Waltham Abbey gunpowder works sat was once part of the abbey estate.

Explosives manufacture is known to have commenced from the mid to late 1600s as a result of increasing demand due to the Third Dutch War of 1672–74. The history of Waltham Abbey is intimately linked to Britain's love affair with getting into fights. Gunpowder was a fickle business, as during the short intervals of peace, black-powder producers had to rely on the mining industry, and when glorious war broke out somewhere, the government demanded a huge increase in production and, more difficult, a uniform and high quality of powder.

Mercifully for the private operators of Waltham Abbey, Britain enjoyed a succession of conflicts including the War of Spanish Succession, the Seven Years' War, numerous wars in India, the American Revolutionary War, the Napoleonic Wars, the War of 1812, the Crimean War ... the list goes on. Through it all, Waltham Abbey's mills kept turning and grinding together the three constituents of charcoal, saltpetre and sulphur.

In the late eighteenth century, Waltham was taken over by the government, and in the aftermath of the French Revolution there was almost continuous demand for munitions. During the War of 1812 (which actually stretched to 1815), the then director of Waltham Abbey, William Congreve, developed a new weapon – a rocket, which was more 'shock and awe' than effective. But its use against the Americans during the naval bombardment of Fort McHenry in 1814 made such an impression that it is mentioned in the American national anthem, 'The Star-Spangled Banner': 'And the rockets' red glare, the bombs bursting in air.'

By the latter half of the nineteenth century, Waltham Abbey was front and centre of the development of chemical-based explosives and propellants, starting with guncotton. Thanks to Alfred Nobel, they also added dynamite and nitroglycerine into the mix. These substances all went bang but too ferociously to be harnessed in a gun or a cannon. With the development of cordite, a composite of guncotton, nitroglycerine and mineral jelly, a major advance in weaponry occurred. Cordite is safe under normal service conditions and it yielded an increased muzzle velocity, ushering projectiles at a greater rate towards the various unfortunates whose country Britain was stealing at the time.

After the Second World War, Waltham Abbey became the only research and development site for non-nuclear explosives, which is nicer, isn't it?

It has a remarkable history, made more significant because the constant change of layout and buildings reflects the astonishing and brutal story of the post-medieval world.

About two days before I closed the filing cabinet for the last time, my curiosity about the number 2 door got the better of me. With heart racing and half-expecting a terrible alarm to go off, I slowly turned the handle and pushed. The bloody thing was open, and I forced it wide to reveal a large aircraft hangar. I was stunned. Every day I had approached the building from an angle that hid the rear of the structure, so I had assumed that it would open up to a small room like the ones I had been working in. Stretching off to the far wall, about fifty metres distant, were rows and rows of old-fashioned timber filing cabinets. Stacked two cabinets, eight drawers high, they formed dim timber-lined corridors. There must have been thousands of them.

I reached for a drawer of the nearest cabinet and it glided out easily. It was jam-packed with thin blue or white papers. I thumbed through and lifted one at random. Topped with the British crest of the lion and unicorn, it was a letter. In a few short, sober lines, it informed a Mr and Mrs Jones that their son had been killed 'somewhere in France' in July 1915. It was signed by the King. I put it back and chose another cabinet and another drawer. It was a similar letter informing a different family that their son was never coming home. I doubled back and went down different aisles. A dozen or so different drawers that I opened contained the same thing. I remember stopping and looking around me in this silent hanger with blue light filtering through dirty skylights above, illuminating the magnitude of the slaughter and sacrifice. I felt like I was crowded into this room with the hundreds of thousands of dead men inscribed on these thin wisps of paper. It seemed such a sad and forgotten place, a halfway house. Neither lost nor found, alive nor dead, just in cold storage. And I felt somehow wrong for disturbing their silence and rudely looking at their personal letters. I moved quickly to the door and closed it behind me but have never forgotten that day.

*

Soon after returning from London, and armed with the site history, we assembled a small team from the Keele and other royal commission offices around the country and travelled to the Waltham Abbey site to start a detailed landscape record.

Working in three teams, we spent fourteen weeks recording every building, feature, ruin, fence post, track and tiniest lump and bump of the seventy-two hectares. It was an extraordinary experience to have the luxury and the time to really look at a landscape. To interrogate it, to squeeze out the last drop of its history, to understand and imagine the hundreds of thousands of actions and events, deliberate and accidental, human and natural, which had occurred over the hundreds of years that it was in service.

It may sound a tedious task, but I never found it so and the experience (together with Hoskins's book) has been the greatest and the most useful influence on my approach to archaeology.

As I mentioned earlier, the Waltham Abbey site was unlike any factory that I have ever encountered. Say the word factory and you may conjure up in your mind rusty buildings and cracked concrete, or perhaps stark, clean processing plants. You probably don't picture fields of rare orchids or dense mature woodland inhabited by deer and picturesque canals wending their way past ruins. But explosives factories, particularly the old ones, are strangely beautiful places.

About halfway through the ground survey, I made the most unusual and gruesome discovery of my career – in a career that has had more than its fair share of the weird and revolting.

It was raining and cold, and the dull afternoon light was making surveying difficult among the denser parts of the woodland that covered the northern half of the site. I was leaning against a tree, listening to the two-way radio and waiting for my survey buddy to disentangle herself from a blackberry patch. Occasionally, the radio crackled into life with an extraordinary string of expletives to inform me that, no, she had not got out yet. I was daydreaming about what I was going to eat for dinner that night when my gaze swept across something buried in the tree trunk. A small pink patch was visible between the rolling folds of tree bark that, given another few years, would have engulfed it entirely. I couldn't make out what it was, so I rubbed my finger over the object to remove some of the green algae and lichen from its surface. When I looked again, I almost fell over with surprise. Grinning back at me was a row of teeth attached to a pale pink gum.

'Cathy, you'd better come and have a look at this,' I said into the radio.

Static and swearing shot back, but it seemed that my partner had untangled herself, and I could see her walking past one of the nitroglycerine mixing houses towards me. She was a tall and willowy Geordie, very good at her job, and swearing, and very funny.

'What?' she said.

I had my hand over the bizarre find in the tree. 'Come and have a look at this.'

She got closer and peered at the back of my hand. 'Well, move your hand, you silly sod.'

I grinned and dropped my hand. There was a moment of puzzlement, then with a satisfying leap backwards, she swore and looked at me.

'There are teeth in that tree.' She said it in an accusatory way, as if I had put them there.

I nodded. 'You don't see that every day, do you?'

A couple of things were immediately clear: the teeth did not belong to the tree and they were not human. They looked human because they were false teeth. The question was how did the top set of false teeth end up buried in the trunk of a beech tree in the middle of a wood at an explosives factory? We looked around and a creeping suspicion began to grow. About thirty metres away, facing the teeth side of the tree, stood the brick-lined entrance through the high blast bank that surrounded the number-two mixing house. I knew the history of this building. In the 1930s three men had been killed in number two. The mixing houses were lightweight structures nestled inside a high earthen bank. These blast banks protected other processing buildings and the people who worked in them by deflecting any explosive force upwards. The buildings were lightweight so that if one went up only splintered timber rained down rather than chunks of brick and mortar.

In those days guncotton and liquid nitroglycerine were mixed together by hand. I know it sounds crazy, but nitro was very sensitive and no machines had been developed that would blend the ingredients without setting it off. So men fitted with elbow-length rubber gloves drew down a prescribed amount of nitroglycerine from lead-lined gutters, which ran directly from the nitro plant some sixty metres away. This emptied into a lead sink that held the guncotton. They then combined the two terrifying ingredients together with a mineral jelly. Once it was fully incorporated, it was amazingly compliant and could stand any amount of rough handling on its way to be extruded into cordite. But something must have happened during the initial drawdown, because the building disintegrated and the three men with it. Not much of the guys was found. It seemed that sixty years on, we had found a little more. It couldn't be a coincidence that dentures were embedded in a tree (that would take some force) directly opposite the only gap in the blast bank that would allow the force of the explosion to travel horizontally.

Subsequently, we dug the teeth out of the tree and they were dated to the right period (yes, there are specialists in this kind of thing), which confirmed what we already knew. It was strange how affected I was by this discovery, considering that I have dug up scores of burials. I guess it was the vivid image that they conjured up of a mercifully quick but unbelievably brutal death.

*

After seven months my contract with the royal commission ended, and I returned to Pembrokeshire with a pretty healthy bank balance and an ambition to spend the summer doing very little besides learning to surf.

I love Pembrokeshire. Other than being my childhood home in the Midlands, its beautiful countryside, mysterious castles and sheltered coves are some of my earliest memories. I'm quite sure I would still be there now and enjoying it immensely if it wasn't for a telephone call out of the blue one sunny afternoon, about two weeks into my endless summer.

The caller was a guy named Bob Watts from the Ministry of Defence. He told me they were preparing to commence remediation and decontamination works on the Waltham Abbey site in preparation for the proposed sale of the land. Located as it was just to the north of London, within the prime commuter belt, it was potentially worth a great deal.

Considering my encyclopedic knowledge of the site, he asked whether I would be interested in consulting to the Ministry of Defence to ensure that significant historic and archaeological elements were protected during the works.

It was another one of those 'I haven't got a clue how to do that' moments, but I didn't let on. 'Yeah, sure, that sounds great.'

He then asked how much money I would want. I had no idea. Archaeologists at that time were notoriously poorly paid. He suggested ten pounds an hour. My brain started racing ... Eighty pounds a day. Eighty pounds a day, you have got to be kidding! That was almost twice the rate for a senior excavation supervisor at that time.

I mumbled, 'That would be fine.' I then asked when he would want me back in London, and he asked where I was living. When he realised I would have to move from Wales to London, he said, 'Oh, we'd better make it fifteen pounds an hour to cover the higher living costs.'

The rest of the conversation was a blur and with many 'thanks' and an 'I'm really looking forward to it', I hung up and danced around my parents' cottage, punching the air and laughing.

The surfing would have to wait. At the tender age of twenty-three, I had just become one of the highest paid archaeologists in the country.

*

A little less than a month later, I was shown to an office with a large window that looked over a weed-choked canal. It contained a metal shelving unit, a filing cabinet, a broad desk under the window, a faded blue swivel chair and a cream-coloured telephone that was placed on a black vinyl tabletop. Bob Watts had the neighbouring office but he was away from the site that morning, and it was the junior project draughtsman who had escorted me from the entrance and shown me where the toilets and kettle and finally my office were.

I stood in the middle of the room, conscious of the fact that not only did I not have a clue what to do, but that I didn't even have a pen.

I sat down and looked out of the window. The desk had drawers to the left and I was partially relieved to find pens, pencils and a pad of notepaper. I wrote a list. I'm a huge fan of lists, the longer the better. I have been known to include tasks such as 'get up' and 'have a coffee' on lists when I've felt particularly unmotivated, so that I would have at least a few things to triumphantly strike off.

There was no job description. The Ministry of Defence didn't know what was required other than they needed an archaeologist on site to ensure the conservation of significant heritage during the extensive decontamination works. I was, however, given a rank. At school I had been an enthusiastic member of the Army Cadet Corps, the school-kid branch of the Worcestershire and Sherwood Foresters Regiment (29th/45th Regiment of Foot), and I'd bloody loved it. Wearing proper uniforms, firing guns, travelling in big noisy trucks, flying in helicopters, riding in battle tanks ... what's not to like?

As I had come closer to graduating from high school, I'd considered a career in the army. I think I would have made a good soldier and am certain that I would have enjoyed it, but I wanted to go to university first and the moment was lost. During my time with the Ministry of Defence, I was given the rank of lieutenant colonel for administrative purposes, which I thought was brilliant. It's only two below a general, and if I'd actually been a lieutenant colonel, I would have commanded a regiment or battalion of about 650 soldiers. As a civilian, it really didn't mean anything apart from sharpening up guards and security at the gates of various bases I would visit.

I was still very young, and while I was a good field archaeologist, I had no experience in managing a project such as this. But with a lot of help from my colleagues at the royal commission and my brother-in-law, Bill, a very experienced archaeologist, I drafted a set of tasks and responsibilities and set forth on the steepest learning curve of my life. (Well, until I had to learn how to present a TV show ... and write a book ... oh, and be a parent.) It was one of the most challenging but most rewarding jobs I have ever had. Every day was different. I learned to make decisions on the wing and collaborate to find solutions to the problems that constantly arose.

On more than one occasion, I was lucky to finish the day in one piece. The closest I have come to dying – properly dying, not just 'Ooh, that was close' – was when I walked into an abandoned factory building and realised, when I reached the middle of its vast space, that I was surrounded by enough really unstable explosive material to mean not only curtains to my young and quite promising life but also that my mortal remains would be handed to my parents in a matchbox.

Strangely, I wasn't particularly scared, possibly because I was young and thought that I was invincible, or possibly because I was in shock. The third possibility, which I think is closer to the mark, is that I was thrilled by the immediate danger. Death doesn't worry me, never has. It's the transition from the state of living (which I enjoy enormously for the most part) to the state of not living that worries me. But here, surrounded by lethal snowdrifts of dry guncotton, I saw that the final journey could be very short and very spectacular.

I looked around at the two older guys with me, who were both rooted to the spot. One was the factory manager, who was turning puce with anger, the other a senior member of the weapons research and development section of the Ministry of Defence – 'Bangs and Flashes' as he called it. He was also an expert in the history of explosives and was all too well aware of what we had just walked into.

Guncotton, or nitrocellulose, is made of cotton fibres, cotton wool or cotton fluff that has been bathed in concentrated nitric and sulphuric acids. The acids bind to the cellulose, adding oxygen and forming an extremely flammable material. Unless it has been completely washed in water to remove any acid, it is a precariously reactive material that can ignite through the slightest percussion or friction, or spontaneously combust if it drops below about 15 per cent water content.

All explosives actually burn, like wood, except they burn very rapidly, giving off an enormous amount of energy in the form of heat and light and also producing a lot of gas. Out in the open, this isn't too much of an issue, and I safely witnessed the disposal of gunpowder and cordite on burning grounds at Waltham Abbey and elsewhere. They burned fiercely, with a lot of smoke but nothing more. Explosives change when the burn is confined by a shell casing or the breach of a gun or, in this case, a great big old brick factory. Then they detonate, and that is a different story.

Geoff the R&D specialist told me to stop moving. He said it in a way that made me obey without question. He could have preceded it with 'If you want to live ...'

I looked around the huge space. There were four two-storey-high timber vats twenty feet to my left, and ahead and to my right were other process structures. Gantries sat idle above us, and looking quite out of place was a large companion desk with all its drawers open to different extents. Blue light filtered in through the dusty skylights in the roof, washing the whole image in a ghostly pallor. And on every surface lay a thick quilt of guncotton. Drifts lay against the pillars of the desk and in the drawers, in the corners of the room, between pieces of equipment. Looking behind, I could see our footsteps in the fine dusting that lay across the floor, and when I looked at my feet the white fluff was stuck to the edges of my boots.

'How much do you think is here?' I asked.

'There could be tons,' said Geoff, who was staring furiously at the factory manager.

He looked back at us both and said, 'Gentlemen, I can only apologise for this. I had no idea. This building should have been decontaminated over six months ago.'

'What would happen if this went up, Geoff?' I remember asking.

'Oh, we would disappear, as would this building. I'd imagine most things within a half mile of here would be flattened.'

We stood there in silence for a moment, contemplating this.

'Well, I think I've probably seen enough. It's a very nice building,' I said. 'So how do we get out of here? I mean, with all our body parts in the same places that they are in now?'

Geoff grinned. 'Well. Don't drag your feet. Very slowly retrace your steps, gently bring each step down as softly as possible. Try not to trip or fall and definitely don't scuff your shoes against the ground. If you do all that, we might get out of this.'

With my heart thumping in my throat, I lifted one foot, turned and placed it slowly, heel to toe, back down on the powdery floor. I looked up at the door twenty metres away and a nervous giggle rose up, which I quickly suppressed. This wasn't a game, this was deadly serious.

The next few drawn-out minutes were how I imagine it would be to walk through a minefield. Not knowing if the next step would be your last. The urge to run was almost irresistable but eventually and with a huge sigh I made it outside and into the sun.

We wiped our feet carefully in the dewy grass in silence. The factory manager set off in a towering rage to the admin building, and Geoff and I followed in slightly more measured gait.

*

One of the achievements I'm most proud of cropped up late one Friday afternoon, when I was notified that the civil engineering team, who were rehabilitating the canal system on site, were planning to drive shutter piles into the canal basin next to the offices. The shutters were thick corrugated steel piles that interlocked, forming a near watertight wall, and these were driven into the base of the canal with a hydraulic vibrating ram.

I swore. I suspected that there was the wreck of a late eighteenth- or early nineteenth-century explosives barge in the basin. Anecdotal accounts placed it hard up against the bank and right in the line of the piling works. The site was of national significance and something such as a 200-year-old wreck would most definitely need to be protected. I tried to call the national body in charge of the heritage protection of the site, English Heritage, but at half-five there was no answer. The piling was programmed to start first thing on the Monday, so I had the weekend to come up with a plan.

What I came up with didn't sound great. In fact, it was likely to fail. The first task was to find the barge, if indeed it was still there, and the second was to figure out a way of raising it before it got smashed to pieces by the piling operation.

The site crew agreed to work on the weekend. By now they had taken on the responsibility of conserving the history of the site and wanted to help me out. So on a chilly Saturday morning, I got into a wetsuit and jumped into the canal to have a feel around in the murky waters for the wreck. I had a snorkel and mask but the water was like soup, so I felt around the squashy canal base with booted feet. Amazingly, I found something almost immediately. I dived down, grabbed the first thing I could hold and dragged it to the surface. A sizeable bunch of guys had gathered on the bank with two big machine excavators at the ready. A bit of a cheer went up when the object that lay in my hand turned out to be a bronze crowbar. It seemed that I had found the wreck. I shuffled around on what felt like the deck in chest-deep water and started to pull up more objects: a bronze spade head, a half-rotten timber pulley block, and then my feet bumped up to what felt like a large bundle of wire. I reached down and dragged the heavy mass out of the mud and onto the bank. The site foreman looked at it and whistled.

It wasn't wire. It was about twenty kilograms of cordite explosive. Yep, I'd definitely found the explosives barge. None of us were concerned about the find. Cordite is a wonderfully stable explosive that takes a lot of coaxing to blow up. And in this condition you'd have to blow it up to ... blow it up.

Before we could attempt to raise the vessel, we would have to clean out all the mud, otherwise it would be too heavy to lift with the machines. So using the two diggers, we curled the huge excavator buckets over and under the far side of the barge and tilted it, so that half of it was out of the water. We hosed out the mud to find that the hull and deck of the barge were in very good condition.

Explosives factories are all designed around reducing the chance of the whole place blowing up. At modern facilities, plastics and other fabrics and materials are employed to eliminate the chance of sparks. Before entering buildings, you are required to check your personal static-charge level, and if it is too high you have to earth yourself. All this effort has produced in the industry some of the safest workplaces in existence. In the past, they had to make do with some weird and wonderful methods. Most metal used as tools or equipment was bronze or lead to eliminate sparks. Workers wore felt-soled shoes and floors were kept scrupulously clean of grit. But the floor surfaces in some of the mixing houses and in the explosives barges were unique. They were made of large tiles of elephant hide tacked down to timber floors with copper nails. Each piece was almost a metre square and a couple of centimetres thick. I was horrified to think about how many poor beasts had been killed to line the factory floors. After the mud was sliced from the barge, we found a few supple elephant-hide tiles still in place.

We cleaned off the mud and I managed to slip a couple of straps around the stern and bow, and with amazing skill, the machine operators slowly lifted the barge out of the canal. It squeaked and groaned, and at one point I thought it was going to snap in half, but we made it in one piece. After photographing and describing its features, we dropped it back into a decontaminated section of canal where it remains to this day. It was the first and only time I have raised a wreck.

My job expanded over the next couple of years, and I found myself advising the ministry on other similar landholdings, so I often travelled the country, nosing around decommissioned and active explosives factories and research bases. One site I visited in southern Scotland had been decommissioned for some time but had recently seen some action. The cordite buildings at this factory were three-storey structures that housed an incredible sorting machine, which processed and sorted different sizes and types of cordite. They were mad-looking objects like something designed by Wallace of *Wallace and Gromit* fame. As well as the complexity of their form, they were impressive because they were entirely made of copper. Unfortunately, this was also the cause of the recent activity.

The site lies on the dunes of a quite remote part of southern Scotland's coast. The caretaker told me, as we drove around the site, that a couple of months before he had discovered a van abandoned at the perimeter fence, and a little further on he noticed one of the cordite buildings was missing a side. The emergency services found the bodies of two guys, together with their acetylene torch. In their rush to pinch the copper, they had forgotten or perhaps didn't realise what the material had been used for.

It was fascinating visiting active sites where bombs were still being made. None of the factories were on any maps, even though they were enormous, and the secrecy didn't stop there. When I chatted to the workers, some of whom had been at a particular site for twenty or more years, they had no idea what happened in other parts of the factory. When I looked incredulously at them, the foreman explained that they didn't allow workers from different process stages to mix – they had separate toilet blocks and mess halls – so that no one had a complete understanding of the bomb-making process. 'Discourages spying,' he said.

I found out on one of these visits that an unpleasant side effect of working in explosives factories, apart from the possibility of being blown sky-high, was 'NG head' or 'bang head'. Exposure to high levels of nitroglycerine causes severe headaches. I remember walking into a process building and being surprised by this overpowering sickly-sweet smell in the air. Within a short time, I was developing a thumping headache. Nitroglycerine is volatile and evaporates readily, and when it's inhaled, its vasodilating effects drop blood pressure and cause this unpleasant sensation. However, the body adapts quickly, so workers habitually exposed experience the headaches only after a weekend or holiday, which means it is also known as the 'Monday morning headache'. To avoid it, some workers took to smuggling small amounts of explosive containing nitroglycerine, such as cordite, out of the factory at the end of a shift. Some would place it in their armpits, while others would pop a wad under their tongue or in their cheek.

Workers who used to handle the most well-known of explosives, TNT or trinitrotoluene, would turn yellow, and during the First World War the mainly female munitions workers were called Canary Girls. Women still form a significant component of explosives manufacture because of their recognised greater attention spans than men's, and because they don't screw up as much (a very good quality in this line of work). It's a miserable industry and the people who worked, and still work, in these places, surrounded by such poisonous and dangerous energy, in full knowledge of the risks, are some of the bravest people I have met.

It's been twenty years since I left my job as archaeological advisor to the Ministry of Defence, but I still consider it as one of the most rewarding and exciting jobs I've ever had. It was such a huge departure from the traditional archaeology career path that I think it allowed me look in all directions and take pretty much anything on.

*

I'd been with the MoD for two and a half years when a gorgeous Australian woman strode into my flat one night with a bottle of red wine in one hand and a bottle of champagne in the other and never left. I hadn't met anyone like Inga. She was beautiful, knowledgeable, smart, sexy, confident and effortlessly adventurous. It really was love at first sight, and when after a couple of months of seeing each other she told me that she had to return to Australia early the following year, I handed in my notice and started packing.

OF DESERT ISLANDS, TIGER SHARKS
AND GOLD-RUSH TOWNS

They're digging in the wrong place!

Indiana Jones, *Raiders of the Lost Ark*, 1981

The beautiful but bleak coast of Western Australia slipped below the wing of the turbo prop plane as I headed north from Perth. I gazed out at the red cliffs and crashing waves and wondered how the hell I had ended up leading a dig to what appeared to be the edge of the world.

I get a lot of industry emails about current excavations, interesting discoveries around the world and archaeology conferences. I often don't have time to read them, but fortunately I'd happened to open one about three months earlier and seen a job advert asking for experienced archaeologists to lead a forthcoming dig. That's not unusual. But what caught my eye was that it was on Dirk Hartog Island in the Indian Ocean. The email had arrived in the middle of a Victorian winter as I was writing a very boring report in a cold and draughty office. I pulled off a glove and picked up the phone.

Dirk Hartog Island forms the western shore of the invitingly named Shark Bay and sits just off the coast of Western Australia, nine hundred kilometres north of Perth. Less than a kilometre of very salty water separates it from mainland Australia at its southern tip, but the north of the long, thin island spears away from the coast into the dark blue of the Indian Ocean.

Named after the Dutch explorer Dirk Hartog, the island is 620 square kilometres of godforsaken scrub, salt pans, towering sand dunes and jagged cliffs. There is no running water, there are no trees and, apart from a small huddle of farm buildings surrounding a single homestead at the south of the island, there are no buildings or roads. It is simultaneously baked by the sun and flattened by the Roaring Forties – south-westerly winds that scream across this remote lump of rock and sand from October to March, rendering it completely uninhabitable.

The beautiful tropical-blue waters to the east seethe with tiger sharks and those to the west boil with deadly currents and constant deep ocean rollers. A holiday island it ain't, which is possibly the reason why Australians aren't munching on salty liquorice while humming, 'I still call New Holland home ...'

Australia could easily have become a Dutch colony, and for many years it was known as New Holland. The Dutch had been accidentally bumping into Western Australia since the early seventeenth century. Some, like Dirk Hartog, who in 1616 arrived at the northern end of the island that now bears his name, survived to tell the tale. Many others literally bumped into the treacherous coast and became some of the first permanent, if dead, European migrants.

Almost all the ships were employed by the Dutch East India Company or the VOC (Vereenigde Oostindische Compagnie), and came across this strange and barren land on their way to the Dutch colonial South-East Asian trading port of Batavia (modern-day Jakarta) on the island of Java. The reason they kept arriving on the West Australian shores was the problem with longitude.

Accurately knowing where one is on the planet at any given moment is now a capability of anyone with a smart phone or a GPS suckered to their windscreen. We hardly give this any thought, but the technology to allow us to track our movements is complex and extremely expensive. There are twenty or so satellites orbiting the earth so that you can find your way to the shops.

The world is divided into lines of longitude that run north–south and lines of latitude that run east–west. During the ages of exploration and expansion of sea trade across the globe, accurate navigation of ocean vessels using longitude and latitude was imperative. But for a long time it was also elusive. Latitude, that is, your location in relation to the equator, could be established quite early on by using sighting instruments (a quadrant or astrolabe) and mapping the location of the sun or fixed stars in relation to the horizon.

Longitude, however, remained stubbornly difficult to measure accurately, especially if you were drifting around on the ocean. Sailors knew where they were in relation to the equator, but out of sight of land they relied on guesswork to estimate where they were around the planet. Dead reckoning was where speed, direction and the time elapsed was used to calculate location in relation to a known start point. But the accurate measurement of time and speed was problematic. Speed on land can be easily determined because land doesn't move around. But on the oceans, currents running independently to a ship made precisely determining speed almost impossible. Reliable time-keeping had always been a problem on ships. Clocks were delicate instruments, and they simply did not work if they were shaken around on a turbulent sea.

To be on the safe side, ships sailed either within sight of land, coasting, or they stuck rigidly to a latitudinal course. There were perils in each. Riding too close to the coast, particularly in storms, ran the risk of wrecking on shoals or reefs. Also, it was often a slow and long way to go. Imagine trying to get from Cape Town to Perth via the coasts of Africa, India and South East Asia. Going along the coast would take many times longer than haring across the middle. But at the same time, heading west or east following a line of latitude could mean running against the winds or currents, making voyage times difficult to estimate, which is not great when you are trying to shop for the trip.

The inability to work out where you were in relation to the Greenwich meridian, or indeed any meridian, was such an issue that the British government established the Board of Longitude in 1714, which set a huge cash prize (equivalent to a million pounds) for anyone who could solve the problem. It took sixty-odd years and some of the best minds in the world to work it out, but eventually it came down to time-keeping. The world is divided into 360 degrees around the equator, and it takes twenty-four hours to rotate completely. Therefore, in one hour it turns fifteen degrees. From an earthly position, the sun traverses the sky by fifteen degrees every hour, and it was the accurate measurement of the position of the sun in relation to the ship and the time that gave longitude.

While this was being sorted out, the VOC, the largest and most profitable company in the world at the time, had its vessels crisscrossing the Indian Ocean with only one coordinate. In an effort to cut the travel time and costs, ships increasingly struck east from the Cape of Good Hope to catch the favourable winds of the Roaring Forties and speed across the Indian Ocean. If they guessed right, they would turn north at the right point and dock at Batavia in good time. If they got it wrong, they smacked into Australia.

For such a rugged and remote landscape, Dirk Hartog Island has a rich past, and in 2006 I was given the opportunity to delve into it. I was commissioned by the maritime archaeology department of the Western Australian Museum to direct excavations on the island with the aim of solving two of the most enduring mysteries in Australian maritime history.

Maritime archaeology, as the name suggests, looks at our endeavours on, or at the least within the sound of, the sea. The main difference between maritime archaeologists and land-based archaeologists is that the former are expected to breathe underwater while on site, whereas the latter generally aren't (mind you, when digging in Britain it is seen as a distinct advantage).

I looked around the cramped cabin of the small regional-airline plane at the team who were joining me on the expedition. All but one were staff of the maritime archaeology department of the museum. The department director, Jeremy Green, was a wild, Hemingway-looking character. Jeremy is one of the pioneers of this relatively young field and took a bit of a gamble employing me, a complete unknown in Western Australia, to lead the digs. He and the other senior staff members (all Brits) had worked together since the 1970s. The remaining member of the team, Bob Sheppard, was an expert metal detectorist who had been working with the museum on and off for years.

We first landed at the tiny airfield of Monkey Mia, which sits on the southern shore of Shark Bay. The connecting flight that would take us onto the island was a single engine, six-seater plane piloted by an enormous Tongan. We looked at each other, at our bags, the pilot and back at the little plane sitting on the tarmac, rocking in the slight breeze. With a bit of huffing and puffing and bag rearrangement, under the doleful gaze of our giant pilot, we all crammed into the plane and then watched as our silent friend carried out some half-hearted checks to the prop and wings before climbing into his seat next to me. The plane lurched to one side and I heard a cracking noise. The pilot's shoulder was above my head and his head was slightly tilted against the cockpit roof. One massive hand worked the controls while the other hung out of the pilot-side window.

The engine sprang to life and the plane slowly started to move. His phone rang as we taxied along the runway, and he jammed the handset in the crook of his neck and started mumbling away. I craned around to look at Jeremy, who seemed completely unconcerned. The others, peeking over the boxes and backpacks on their laps, were slightly pale. Without withdrawing his arm into the cockpit or ceasing the phone call, our pilot revved up the engine till it was howling and started bumping down the runway. If it hadn't been for the fact that I was convinced we were going to die, it would have been hilarious.

Of course, he knew what he was doing and we cleared the airport perimeter fence with centimetres to spare. It was a beautiful day with a clear blue sky, and the water of Shark Bay sparkled in the late morning sun. It was so clear I spotted a pair of manta rays, each the size of a two-car garage, flapping off to the north, and of course sharks, lots of sharks. The island came into view almost immediately, and I started scanning for the runway but couldn't see anything. As we took a slow loop around a low headland, I spotted a purple-dusted salt pan where the scrub had been pushed aside to create a narrow strip. As the plane dipped towards it, I started to swear. Mercifully, the pilot had finished his call by then and we landed in a cloud of dust and lurched to a stop at a small bus stop–like shelter of wind-etched timber and torn green shade cloth. An upturned white plastic chair completed the Dirk Hartog Island Airport terminal building.

Half of the team had driven from Perth in two four-wheel-drives and, together with trailers, had taken the small barge across from the mainland to the southern tip of the island, not far from where we landed.

I'd been in isolated places before, but when the plane took off and returned towards the east, I felt like I'd been marooned on a desert island. Oh, wait … it was a feeling that only increased as the day went on. A two-and-a-half-hour slow and bumpy drive eventually brought us to a small corrugated-iron shack that was to be our expedition camp for the next three weeks. It was located on the north-western shoulder of the island and, perched on a sandy bluff, the shack overlooked low dunes and a rugged platform of rock carved into peaks and gullies by the constant waves that thudded against it.

It was beautiful and really felt like the edge of the earth. I was filled with the sudden flush of energy that you get when you realise you are on an adventure and living something unique.

For the next three weeks that feeling did not leave me and I enjoyed every moment. We lived a strange existence, camping in the sand dunes and using the shack as a canteen, office, meeting room and bar. The barrels of fresh water that we'd brought with us were for drinking and cooking only, so we bathed in the rock pools. Here the sea floor drops quickly, and large pelagic fish and deep-sea creatures are found within a very short distance from shore. Within moments of getting out of the four-wheel-drive and gazing out to sea, I saw my first whale. Only thirty to forty metres offshore, a huge humpback whale lurched out of the water. It pirouetted in the air, waving its oarlike and ungainly pectoral fins skyward before crashing in a huge cloud of spray back beneath the surface. Every day I watched this amazing dance as scores of whales on their migration south swept past, thumping their tails and slapping the water with their pectoral fins. They would jump and twist in pairs, sometimes with their young. Or they would startle you with a loud blast of spray from their blowholes or would simply cruise past on their sides, with one huge eye looking at you. The experience of bathing in a warm rock pool with whales playing at my feet as the sun touched the horizon was extraordinary.

*

The first excavation was one of the most curious and complex that I have ever carried out. Not far from the camp lay Turtle Bay, a stunning crescent beach backed by a steep cliff rising perhaps forty metres above the shore. To the west is Cape Inscription, the imaginatively named cape where inscriptions were left by Dirk Hartog and a subsequent Dutch explorer, Willem de Vlamingh.

Apparently the Dutch were not the only people interested in this desert island. Somewhere on the plateau immediately above

Turtle Bay, a French aristocrat – le Comte de Saint-Aloüarn – claimed Western Australia for King Louis XV. My job was to find the papers of annexation that, it was recorded, were placed in a wine bottle that was sealed with a coin, encased in lead and buried. Somewhere. In 1772. I looked across the scrub and sand that stretched along the top of the steep ridge behind the beach towards Cape Inscription. With no discernible features on the surface, we were going to have to rely on the maps drawn by Saint-Aloüarn over 230 years before. An image of a huge pile of hay and a small needle came to mind.

To complicate matters, ours wasn't the first attempt to locate the annexation bottle. Ten years before, the museum had indeed found a bottle of the right age but it was empty. Prior to that search, there were accounts of a bottle being recovered by a farmer who lived on the island, and it was claimed that this one had held the letter of annexation but had perished in a fire at the homestead sometime later.

So really my task was to either find the bottle and letter, and therefore recover a highly significant artefact and disprove the farmer theory, or recover evidence to prove the farmer theory and show that the bottle wasn't there anymore. While this sounds difficult – and I was momentarily nervous – this type of challenge is what archaeology is all about, because looking at the soils (or in this case sand) during excavation can tell you a lot about what, if anything, has happened in the past. Archaeology is as much about soils as it is about the artefacts that lie in them. Evidence of soil disturbance, by someone digging around for a bottle for instance, can be seen hundreds or thousands of years after the event. Variations, such as changes in the compaction and colour or even the smell of soils, can highlight past activities.

During the previous expedition, the archaeologist had excavated small trenches where Bob the metal detectorist had identified a metal object, and by luck they had found a bottle. But small postbox-sized trenches cannot provide a clear understanding of the nature of the soils across a landscape. I decided that to be successful we would need to look for evidence of pits or other disturbance, and to do that we needed to dig bigger trenches … much bigger. On the first morning when I suggested that we dig a couple of five by five trenches across the study area, the team of maritime archaeologists looked a bit despondent, dropping the big tape measures that they had been holding and picking up small rulers. Momentarily puzzled, I soon realised that they had thought I meant five centimetres squared. When I clarified my intent as metres, everyone beamed and set to work setting up the string lines to outline the trenches. Clearly, they were as keen as I was to clear up this mystery.

Over the next ten days, we carefully excavated sections of the landscape that according to Saint-Aloüarn's own notes were where he had buried the bottle and annexation note. And while the metal detector found hundreds of metal objects (mostly corroded fencing wire and beer-can ring-pulls), no evidence of the bottle or its contents were found until, near the end of the dig, we uncovered some dark green glass fragments in an area of disturbed soil. These tiny and insignificant artefacts and churned-up ground were the pieces of the puzzle that we had been looking for. We had solved the mystery after 230 years.

These glass shards were the remaining fragments of the French wine bottle deposited in 1772, and the disturbed ground showed that the bottle had been excavated and broken open to get to the letter. But it was the discovery of a simple aluminium (or tin) ring pull in the disturbed soil next to the bottle pieces that showed the bottle had been discovered relatively recently. This was support for the story of the farmer finding France's brief – and, it has to be said, half-hearted – declaration of sovereignty over the bleak shores of Western Australia.

*

For over a week, we had been entertained and amazed by the acrobatics of the humpback whales that passed the beach and by the extraordinary manta rays that ponderously flapped their way across the bay. But it was the tiger sharks that most fascinated and horrified me.

Every day a small group of tiger sharks would cruise into the bay and start herding shoals of fish towards the beach. With lightning-fast movements, their slick forms would head off the fish trying to escape these encircling killers. The shore break would then erupt in a frothing mass of silver as the sharks charged into their target, mouths gaping wide. Often they would beach themselves and for a moment would thrash around on the wet sand, before using their pectoral fins to shuffle back into the water. These were big sharks, two to three metres long, and they did this every day.

I found myself holding my breath as I watched, and when it was over, my heart would be racing. So when one of the team suggested we go for a bit of a snorkel one lunchtime, I burst out laughing. But everyone else thought that was a great idea. I looked from one to the other but no one seemed to be kidding.

'But the sharks,' I said incredulously, pointing to the water below.

'We'll be right, they seem pretty well fed. They're not likely to bother us,' one of the group told me as he dug out his swimmers from a backpack.

Then I remembered I was surrounded by maritime archaeologists. These guys lived in the water. Some, I suspect, even had gills. Maybe it was an initiation thing for me. They were working in my territory, on land. Perhaps they wanted to show me their domain. Whatever the reason, it was the craziest suggestion I had ever heard.

I'd had a close encounter with a shark seventeen years before and the experience still made me shiver. I'd been working on an Iron Age site on a small island in the Persian Gulf, close into the coast of the Emirate of Umm al-Quwain. Lying to the north of Dubai, it is the least populous of the seven emirates that make up the United Arab Emirates. Me and a small team of archaeology students from the Institute of Archaeology were surveying a low island as part of an expedition to the huge pre-Islamic site of Al-Dour, a hugely important trading port during the Persian period about two thousand years ago. One day we had been walking over the island for hours in the sun and we decided to have a dip in the shallow lagoon that stretched between us and the mainland, less than half a kilometre away. The water was beautiful and refreshing and crystal clear. Everyone had got out and I was slowly swimming back in when one of my mates pointed over my shoulder and shouted, 'Shark!'

'Yep. Very funny,' I shot back, not even bothering to look over my shoulder. But then a couple of others stood up and started shouting for me to get out of the water. I looked over my shoulder and there was the unmistakable dorsal fin of a shark about twenty metres behind me.

I was in chest-deep water about fifteen metres from shore. I didn't know whether to swim or run so I did both. It was an awful feeling. Panic was rising and I was sure that any moment I was going to be pulled under by rows of sharp teeth. It wasn't helping that by now the whole team were shrieking at me to swim faster and saying useful things like, 'It's getting closer.'

I made the shore and lay heaving on the sand, trying not to vomit. I turned to the water and saw the fin slide under the surface less than ten metres away. I have no doubt that if it had wanted to, it could have got me in a second. It was a very nervous trip back to the mainland on our tiny inflatable dinghy.

Foolishly, back at Turtle Bay I decided I didn't want to appear chicken, and thought that this might be a good opportunity to face my fears. It wasn't. Once snorkelled and masked up, I walked into the bay and dropped below the surface. The water was warm and clear, and small amounts of coral clung to a rocky reef just off the beach. Colourful fish darted around everywhere and it was all very nice. But while the others were ducking and diving around, exploring among the rocks, I was hyperventilating and trying to swim in a casual way, all the time looking around for the menacing grin of a tiger shark looming out of the blue. After about ten minutes, a shoal of large silver fish, just like the ones targeted by the sharks, came swimming very quickly towards us like something was chasing them. Fish have eyes that look like they are surprised or scared all the time. So having a hundred of them streaming towards me, looking like they were crapping themselves, was enough for me. I froze as they bolted to either side of me, waiting for the toothy menace to appear.

Nothing was behind them, but I was out of there. Interestingly, everyone else got out at the same time and no one suggested a swim again.

*

The second excavation on Dirk Hartog Island was another French site, around the northern tip of the island to the east of Turtle Bay. Seventy years after Saint-Aloüarn's visit, the French whaling ship *Persévérant* was wrecked on the north-eastern point of the island when the ship dragged its anchor in a storm.

No lives were lost in the wrecking but, as I mentioned before, Dirk Hartog Island is halfway between nowhere and bugger all, and that's in the twenty-first century. In 1841, after the storm subsided, the crew found themselves marooned on a true desert island beyond the horizon of any shipping. *Persévérant* had been at sea for almost six months and the crew were not having a good time. Packed to the gunwales with whale oil, baleen and blubber, she was a floating fortune, but the men on board were suffering the age-old disease of the sea: scurvy.

Its almost non-existence in the modern world means that it no longer imparts the same fear as it should. Scurvy is a dreadful disease. It is estimated to have been responsible for the deaths of over two million sailors during the three hundred years prior to the nineteenth century, scary results from a prolonged dietary deficiency of vitamin C. On long voyages, the lack of fresh food and a diet heavy on dried meat and grains made scurvy a common condition. Without treatment it is invariably fatal but not until the scorbutic victim has experienced a laundry list of horrible symptoms. First they would feel very tired. Then, as the disease progressed, they would experience bone and muscle pains, then difficulty breathing followed by spongy and bleeding gums. Then their teeth would start falling out. Towards the end, they would go mad and eventually succumb to fevers, fits and then curtains.

It wasn't until the 1930s that a link was confirmed between vitamin C and scurvy, even though it was known that fresh fruit and vegetables alleviated the symptoms, and by the 1870s it was a requirement on Royal Navy ships and common practice on others to carry citrus juice on long voyages. The term 'limey' was coined by Americans for British sailors based on the practice of daily lime juice being handed out on ships.

It appeared that the crew of *Persévérant* were unaware of this preventative. The young Captain Duval directed the ship to Shark Bay, where he hoped to cure the crew with supplies of fresh fish and turtle. However, by the time he reached the northern tip of Dirk Hartog Island, eight crew were sick with scurvy and the ship's rudder required repairs. While the sick were being tended to on the island by the surgeon, *Persévérant* was caught in a storm that caused it to drag its anchor and be carried around the point stern-first towards a series of shoals about three hundred metres offshore. Duval ordered the mizzen mast to be cut down to lighten the ship and raise it over the shoals. But as it did so in howling wind and rain, the rudder was ripped from the hull and water flooded into the hold. Driven by the wind and waves, the ship was pushed onto the beach and stuck fast.

The crew were all alive, but that was the best they could say of the situation. The uninhabited island was a long way east of traditional whaling grounds and trade routes, their ship was beyond repair and there wasn't a lemon in sight.

When the storm abated, they unloaded their cargo and supplies and established a camp in the dunes behind the beach, waiting for a ship that I am sure they knew would never arrive. How do I know all this? Well, after ten weeks on the island, with five of the crew dying of scurvy and the remainder in deteriorating health, they decided to set sail for Java in four pirogues (small boats used to pursue and harpoon whales). Two of the four boats didn't survive the journey, but Duval made it to Batavia and from there took the long journey home to France, where he had to face an inquiry. It's from those records that we know the fate of the *Persévérant* and its crew.

*

The aim of the dig was to shed light on how the crew survived in such desperate circumstances for so long. I also wanted to discover what life was like in the survivors' camp and, if possible, locate the final resting places of the five crew who died during their enforced island holiday.

It was such a wildly adventurous story and when, with great difficulty, we arrived at the site, it revealed itself to be a suitably dramatic location. The site lay between the fore dunes and a larger line of secondary dunes behind one of the most beautiful beaches I've ever seen. A short distance to the north was a low promontory that marked the northern tip of the island. To the south, the white sand beach and grey-green sand dunes stretched for miles to disappear into the shimmering heat.

However, the feeling of isolation overwhelmed me. It didn't take much imagination to place myself in the story, because it didn't look like anything had changed in 165 years. The dunes may have moved a bit, and the vegetation had come and gone, but there were no modern structures such as power poles or roads to impinge on the scene.

In front of us lay a broad scatter of artefacts – barrel hoops, broken glass and pottery – mute and evocative evidence of a brief and desperate interlude. This was what I'd gotten into archaeology for. Way back when, as a seven-year-old, I wanted to know the story of the monk. And almost thirty years later, I had the opportunity to speak for the dead and tell their tale, the final act for some of the actors and a life-altering one for the others. Of all the projects I have worked on, I think this site was the most moving. And I hate whaling.

Whereas the Saint-Aloüarn site had been all about the soils, the *Persévérant* survivors' camp was all about the artefacts. A few quickly excavated test pits showed that the site had no subsurface deposits; that is, there were no artefacts or archaeological evidence below the surface. Before we disturbed the artefact scatter by stomping over the soft dune surface, we recorded everything with high-resolution photography, and then we got on our hands and knees and searched, identified and recorded every recognisable artefact.

Over the years, the site had been degraded by natural factors such as corrosion and erosion, and human activity had also affected its integrity. While the area is remote, a small number of sports fishermen make it up to the northern point of the island every year, and a four-wheel-drive track cut across the site closest to the beach. There is no doubt that interesting artefacts have been collected by visitors.

However, each piece was a fragment of the tale of the *Persévérant*'s crew. We discovered the corroded fragments of a desalination boiler, which solved how they got water. Arrangements of barrel hoop showed where they had stacked their supplies and perhaps where they sheltered from the wind and the sun. We found buttons marked with a 'fouled' anchor (an anchor wrapped with rope) and the term Equipage de Ligne, which showed that some of the crew were ex-French navy. And we found a tooth and a skull fragment to remind us that some of the crew never left.

By the end of the dig, I was sad to leave this island on the edge of the world but also humbly satisfied. It had been ten years since arriving in Australia, and as I flew over Shark Bay on my way back to Perth, I felt that at last I was hitting my stride and doing the kind of archaeology that I wanted to do: the kind that put the experience of our ancestors, recent and distant, front and centre.

*

I had arrived in Australia one cloudy and cool February day in the mid-1990s, in love and with about four thousand pounds in my bank account and once again without a bloody clue what I was going to do.

My friends reckoned being an archaeologist in Australia was like being a tree surgeon in the Sahara. In Victoria in the mid-1990s this wasn't far off. The archaeological industry was very different from the UK. When I say different, I mean almost non-existent. Heritage was a dirty word at the time, as Melbourne was experiencing a construction boom under a pro-development state government. The few consultancies that were in Victoria had no room and less interest in sharing a slice of a very small pie with a young Englishman, who, I have to admit, was probably pretty cocky, coming as I did from one of the best archaeology jobs in the UK.

So I hit a big stone wall, career-wise. Heritage Victoria were kind enough to throw me some artefact drawing work, but apart from that, nothing. When Inga had completed the last part of her nursing degree, six months after we arrived in Australia, we decided to spend a year travelling around the country for no particular reason other than that there was nothing stopping us. Apart from a small dig in Darwin, where I helped a PhD student excavate some shell middens, there was no archaeological work to be had anywhere. During the 27,000-kilometre trip I did learn how to be a barista, how to clean toilets and how to avoid being eaten, bitten, stung and killed horribly by Australia's terrifying natural fauna and flora (the stinging tree in northern Queensland is definitely to be feared).

On our return to Melbourne a year later, the archaeological work situation was, if anything, worse, and I ended up taking whatever job I could. I worked as a pushbike courier (neck-to-ankle lycra and very sore legs), a market researcher for oil companies (being chased off petrol-station forecourts by suspicious station managers) and, best of all, painting the Anzac-class frigates at the docks in Williamstown in Melbourne (mostly grey).

All of this was fine, but my career was going backwards, and after two years it was looking increasingly likely that we would have to head back to the UK. But then I got a job. It was a small consultancy project for the Victorian Department of the Environment. As part of their fire management plan for the Victorian Alpine region, they asked me to locate about fifty historic sites that had been recorded in the area but had not been visited or assessed. Take the list, find the site on the ground and record it. They would even throw in a four-wheel-drive on top of my fee. It sounded simple.

It wasn't. The Victorian Alps are some of the wildest and remotest landscapes in Australia. The map references that came with the site lists were vague, at best to the nearest square kilometre. That wouldn't be too bad if I had been looking for an old house in some fields, but I was looking for small holes in the ground or tumbled-down miner's or timber-getter's shacks in the midst of impenetrable old-growth forest. I spent weeks camping alone in the increasingly chilly mountains, my tent pitched on fire tracks, often with menacing packs of wild dogs keeping me company on the autumn nights. I hadn't even known there were wild dogs in Australia, but there are lots of them, and they are all rather big and hang around in gangs, picking off marsupials, lambs and archaeologists.

One day I looked at my list and saw that the next site I had to find was a sawdust heap. I stopped on a muddy logging track and thought that perhaps I'd reached the lowest point in my archaeological career. A sawdust heap. Quite apart from the daunting prospect of trying to find a heap of sawdust in the middle of a forest the question was: why bother looking for it in the first place? If it still existed. Then I looked up and the largest sawdust heap I have ever beheld sat steaming in the morning sun, covering about an acre of the forest floor. Oh.

While this job was tricky, it was fun and a welcome change from sitting around in a pokey Victorian worker's cottage in North Carlton, feeling sorry for myself. Mountains always make me feel good, and I was exercising and it was a job.

I'd been camping beside the Mitta Mitta River for about a week when the local police officer from the village of the same name made the short walk to my tent. I'd been at his house for a barbecue a few nights before, where I had met his family and half the village, so I wasn't alarmed by his arrival.

'You've got a phone call at the station,' he said. Remember those days without mobiles? 'Something about you needing to go to Sydney as soon as possible for a job interview.'

This was news to me, but by the next evening I was on the Albury overnight train to Sydney in my least stained and rumpled clothes. Within the month, Inga and I were living in central Sydney, where I had got a job as an archaeologist with an environmental firm, and Inga at Sydney Hospital. For the first time since leaving London we were both earning.

My job was to do survey work and report writing for the environmental consultancy, which I carried out for a few years, but I hankered to get back out in the field.

So in 1999 I set up my own company, DIG International, with the intention of getting back to excavation. For at least the first couple of years I continued to do more desk-based planning-style archaeological work for government bodies such as the New South Wales Government Architects, Roads and Traffic Authority and as the City Archaeologist for the City of Sydney Council. They were good solid jobs, and I got to work with great people and learn valuable business skills, but open-plan offices were a far cry from the archaeological adventures that I loved.

Inga and I had both of our daughters while we were living in a little flat in Bondi Beach, and suddenly the city that had been so much fun was now a thousand kilometres away from the nearest grandparents and family. So we returned to Inga's home town, Ocean Grove, a little holiday village at the mouth of the Barwon River on the Victorian south coast. With two children, a mortgage, a rapidly receding hairline (mine) and no work for either of us, it didn't seem like the best idea but at least we had babysitters. As it turned out we would need them.

As soon as we landed in Victoria I started picking up work, and within a couple of months I was preparing to direct my first excavation in Australia. The dig was in the great goldfields city of Bendigo, an hour to the west of Melbourne, and it was the start of a long connection with the city.

I first heard the city's strange name as a child. I knew nothing else about it, just the name, uttered by my parents together with the equally alien names of Cape Town and Vancouver. In the first decades postwar, Commonwealth countries, particularly Canada, South Africa and Australia, were crying out for skilled migrants to rebuild the nations. Dad, a civil engineer, could have picked up a job and a passport in any of those countries with ease. He didn't take the leap in the end and remained in the Black Country, becoming a lecturer at a university in Birmingham.

But, of course, thousands did take the gamble – and not only in the 1950s but a hundred years earlier, at the beginning of the extraordinary history of Bendigo. One of the most challenging sites I dug was in the centre of Bendigo on Forest Street. I was partly attracted to this field out of a voyeuristic curiosity to peer into the past … to rummage, poke and prod into the private lives of people who I will never meet, but on whose shoulders we all stand. I also wanted to dig stuff up, and the Forest Street excavation certainly satisfied these urges.

The dig was as complex an archaeological site, in terms of overlaying and intercutting occupation deposits, as any in Australia and presented challenges comparable with those on urban archaeological sites in London, Rome or New York.

Archaeological sites are made up of essentially two elements, artefacts and soils. Generally, it's the careful observation of soil layers, or strata, that tells the archaeologist how the site was created and the sequence of past occupation. In an ideal sequence of soil layers, the surface strata is the latest or youngest and the deepest soil deposit is the earliest or oldest.

But, of course, in reality things are not quite that simple, and features such as pits and privies (toilets), wall foundations and service trenches intrude on earlier soil layers. As well as muddling the picture of the earlier deposits, material taken from these layers ends up on upper occupation surfaces as the labourer throws the soil from the foundation trench he's digging to one side. Not only will we have vertical disturbances to our pretty layer cake, but also vertical movement of artefacts. So if you rely on dating the occupation sequence of a site by analysis of the artefacts alone, you can get into all sorts of trouble. Therefore looking at the dirt becomes as important.

An additional problem occurs when the soil layers are thin or are of the same colour as the layers above and below. This was the rather messy picture presented to us at Forest Street and is, of course, the typical picture created by the dynamic cycle of construction, renovation, adaptation, demolition and reconstruction that you see around any urban landscape. The extraordinary nature of the boom-and-bust history of Bendigo meant that these urban deposits formed over a very short period of time.

Sites such as Forest Street keep archaeologists on their toes – and that's fun, if slow going. Forest Street clearly demonstrated the rich resource that lay beneath and showed that Bendigo, throughout the gold rush, built upon itself in a constant and relentless effort to renew, adapt and remain relevant.

The first Australian gold rush started in New South Wales in April 1851, but strikes were made in Victoria in the same year. The Victorian rushes of the 1850s in Ballarat and Bendigo wrought profound changes to the colony's economy and the greater economy of the British Empire. Such was the allure, the road to the gold diggings was a mile wide in places, as thousands of people walked off farms and out of respectable jobs to seek their fortune. Forty of the forty-two police officers of the small town of Melbourne deserted their positions and headed west. A hundred ships lay at anchor at Melbourne's docks, stranded because there were no crews to man them because they had all high-tailed it to the muddy creeks.

People also travelled from around the world to seek their fortunes. The Chinese, fleeing the depredations of the Opium Wars, came in their hundreds and brought a new distraction to the miners, opium. Americans and all the nationalities that had worked the Californian gold rush of the 1840s crossed the Pacific to continue their hunt for the big strike. The alluvial gold found on the Victorian fields was particularly rich. In the early days, guys were just picking nuggets off the surface.

Bendigo grew from nothing to a significant town in a couple of years. One of the notable characteristics of the artefacts recovered from my digs was the high proportion of expensive goods, such as fine dinnerware, champagne bottles by the barrowload and oyster shells by the shovelful. Bendigo in the summer gets hot, really very hot, and I recoiled from the thought of what state those oysters would have been in by the time they had journeyed up from Melbourne on horse and cart, without refrigerated transport.

But no, after a bit of research, it turns out that the oysters and other fine delicacies arrived in pristine condition, packed in ice. The remarkable thing is that the ice had come from North America. Sawn from the frozen lakes and streams of New England, Maine and Wisconsin in winter, it was cut into large blocks, and then loaded onto ships and packed in straw or sawdust to slow its melting. Then the ships sailed across both the Atlantic and Indian oceans to arrive at Melbourne.

It's incredible, but the ice trade centred on the American east coast supplied most of the ice for the world during the nineteenth century. In the latter half of that century, the trade employed 90,000 people and made the equivalent of over half a billion dollars. Due to Australia's ridiculous distance from the chilly frozen ponds of New England (resulting in the equally silly wastage of ice, with often 50 per cent melting en route),

Melbourne was one of the first places in the world to establish a commercially viable ice-making plant.

All this gold and wealth brought others who set up all forms of entertainment and shops to part the weary miners and their treasure. Melbourne developed from a small town of around 12,000 people, at the beginning of the 1850s, to a seething and sophisticated metropolis of over 200,000 a decade later.

The Bendigo gold rush can be seen in two phases: the chaotic and romantic alluvial rush, when any man with a shovel and a willingness to dig some dirt had the chance to strike it rich; and the second phase, when all the alluvial deposits had been sifted, and the mining corporations took over and chased the seams underground. Cornish miners, experts in deep-reef mining, were brought in to establish the gold mines that would honeycomb the earth beneath Bendigo. Many of these immigrants arrived with their families and their Wesleyan faith.

In 2006 I excavated a couple of sites that showed the changing nature of the goldfields. The sites were no more than three hundred metres apart along Golden Gully, the creek where gold was first discovered in 1851. But they may as well have been poles apart. Excavations at the first site revealed a modest but well-built stone cottage set inside a walled compound, with outbuildings including a laundry and a small paved courtyard. Finds of fine Staffordshire dinnerware and personal items showed that a family with children had lived here in the second half of the nineteenth century. One exceptional discovery was a leather hat discovered on the floor of the cottage. Not unlike a trilby, it had a small patch of wax stuck to the leather of the narrow brim. Historic photographs show identical hats worn by workers down the gold mines with short candles fixed to their brims to illuminate the way. I say that this find was exceptional because objects made of organic materials, such as leather, do not survive very well in archaeological contexts. While there are plenty of examples where wood, cloth and even bodies are preserved for thousands of years, these are most unusual, and generally, archaeological evidence is heavily skewed to inorganic and enduring objects such as pottery and stone.

On the subject of skewed artefact collections, this site was unique in that we didn't find any alcohol bottles or tobacco pipes. On every other goldfield site I have worked on, there has been copious evidence of previous occupants living it up. There is a very important phrase to remember when one is analysing archaeological evidence: the absence of evidence is not the evidence of absence. But in this case the artefacts reflected the true nature of the family who lived within this Wild West landscape 140 years or so ago. They were Wesleyan Cornish, and, as such, both the adults would have signed The Pledge. This was a formal promise to abstain from booze and smokes, and our discoveries reflected their piousness.

The second site couldn't have been more different. It was located on the bank of Golden Gully on a level field and consisted of two ramshackle huts, a couple of outbuildings and a lot of rubbish. The soil here was thick and rich, unlike anywhere else on the Victorian goldfields where the topsoil had been washed away during the frantic search for surface gold. Checking against historical accounts of the area, I discovered that there was a market garden along the gully in the 1860s. That would explain the good topsoil.

As we continued to dig, we discovered a collection of artefacts very different from the first site. There were large piles of broken alcohol bottles just outside the entrances to the little shacks. The shacks were roughly made, with some sections built of stone and others that appeared to be repaired with pieces of tin. Then we discovered two artefacts that gave us the identity of our market gardeners. One was a largish piece of pottery of a beautiful pale turquoise blue and the other was a flattened piece of tin with the impression of a dragon decorating it. The first was a piece of rice bowl, made in China, and the other was part of a package that contained opium. Accounts mention a number of market gardens in the area but only one was run by Chinese – the Fong brothers – and these artefacts proved that this was their property. It is the presence of the rice bowl more than the opium tin that is the conclusive evidence, because there are almost no instances where oriental ceramics, such as rice bowls, are found in European occupation deposits. It just doesn't happen. And it wasn't just the cultural objects of Chinese and non-Chinese that didn't mix; nor did the communities. The Chinese, an important and vibrant part of the goldfields community, were kept isolated with apartheid regulations that dictated where they could work and trade and live. The majority of Bendigo's Chinese lived in a number of camps. In the evenings, curfews restricted their movements outside these camps but didn't curtail the stream of Europeans visiting the opium dens within them.

The importation and use of opium was an open and legal trade in the nineteenth century, but again, while Europeans visited opium dens, there are few examples of opium paraphernalia found within European archaeological deposits.

I imagined a picture of our pious Cornish family dressed in their Sunday finest averting their eyes as they passed by their drug-smoking, hard-drinking foreign neighbours.

The discovery of gold was perhaps the single most significant event in the early development of Australia. It changed the population, the towns, the cities and the national character. The campaigns for improved miners' rights led to universal suffrage and a revolution of the democratic rights and workers' privileges across the country. The wealth generated from the Victorian goldfields developed Australians' self-belief and self-reliance and an optimistic energy that saw the country through the depressions and wars that followed. The sites that I excavated showed glimpses of the precarious but wildly adventurous lives of the people who played a part in nation building.

Recall the Ann Jones inn at Glenrowan, scene of the famous Kelly Gang siege, which looms large in Australia's history. I mentioned at the beginning of this book I had the honour to dig it.

OF BUSHRANGERS, BLOODY CODES AND BULLETS

... the horsemen passed in silence, scarcely deigning to look round.
Heavy men and large of stature, reckless how they bore their guns,
or how they sate their horses, with leathern jerkins, and long boots,
and iron plates on breast and head, plunder heaped behind their
saddles, and flagons slung in front of them; I counted more than
thirty pass, like clouds upon a red sunset.

RD Blackmore, *Lorna Doone: A Romance of Exmoor*

The Ned Kelly story, particularly the siege at Glenrowan and Ned Kelly's last stand, is unique in Australian history in that it is well known both throughout the country and across the world. The story has evolved from historical fact to myth and legend and is widely acknowledged as significantly contributing to the Australian national identity; it is imbued with qualities that Australians admire, including larrikinism and mateship. Conversely, the Kelly story shows the problems of a class system adopted from the 'old countries' of Britain and Ireland. It encompasses a life of poverty and disparity in a society riven by religious prejudice, as experienced by many in nineteenth-century Australia.

The dig was particularly challenging because the Kelly story has for years been bleached by the spotlight until, like an old Polaroid, it is difficult to see the picture clearly anymore. Historical accounts are often incomplete but, more importantly, they are often inaccurate. They are biased towards the victor, the government or the morality of the prevailing society, or even just the nature of the author. This is very true in the case of the Kelly legend. In fact, it's difficult to think of a history that has been more revised and rewritten, pawed and pored over than the Kelly story. So much has been written (five hundred books at last count), dramatised and eulogised that the real story is beyond reach and, for some, beyond caring.

The Kelly legend has a polarised following. To some, the gang members, and particularly Ned Kelly, are considered to be chancers, thieves and cold-blooded murderers whose rhetoric about class and Irish Catholic persecution was just an attempt to justify their crimes. Others regard him as a hero of the downtrodden. The iconic image of Ned returning terribly wounded into the fray in an attempt to rescue his brother and friend is the quintessential picture of Australian mateship and was a story exploited by the Australian propaganda machine during the First World War.

Without the siege, the Kelly Gang may have slipped into history as a bunch of bloodthirsty young bushrangers and sat alongside other partly remembered outlaws such as Harry Power and Captain Moonlite in the Australian gallery of rebels. But the siege did happen, and at the Glenrowan Inn the Kelly legend was born.

This situation provided both an opportunity and a challenge to the archaeological project. The opportunity was to add fact and substance to the legend. The challenge was to conduct the project as impartially and sensitively as possible. Directing a large archaeological project is stressful enough without the Sword of Damocles hanging over your head, ready to be wielded by one Kelly side or the other.

It was clear from my meeting with the local constabulary that the story of the Kelly Gang was too recent for us to be flippant or cavalier about the dig. This story unfolded within the lifetimes of the locals' grandparents and great-grandparents. It's not folklore yet and there are people alive who are still bloody angry about the whole affair. So I was keen to see if an archaeological approach could shed a different, perhaps unbiased light on the incident.

Before I could get on site I had to do a significant amount of historical research. First, I needed to understand the story, the historical context that would help me to decide which archaeological elements were significant and why. Second, I had to find out which archaeological deposits were likely to have survived under the unassuming, overgrown house block.

Ned's capture, and the slaying of his brother Dan and friends Joe and Steve during the last major gun battle on Australian soil, ended a notoriety that had captured the collective imagination of Australians for two years. The Kelly Gang, as Ned Kelly, Dan Kelly, Steve Hart and Joe Byrne became known, emerged in the public consciousness in 1878 when they murdered three police officers at Stringybark Creek. The story of the gang began, however, with the birth of its leader, Edward (Ned) Kelly in 1854 at Beveridge, north of Melbourne, to John 'Red' Kelly and Ellen Kelly.

Red Kelly was an Irishman who had been convicted of criminal acts and sentenced to seven years of penal servitude, then transported to Tasmania, arriving in 1843. There is uncertainty surrounding the exact nature of his crimes, as most of Ireland's court records were destroyed during the Irish Civil War. Some sources say he stole livestock, others that he was a political prisoner. Red moved to Victoria in 1848 after gaining early release and found work in Beveridge at the farm of James Quinn, another Irish immigrant. Red married Quinn's daughter Ellen in 1850. Red was thirty and Ellen was eighteen. They had six children, with Ned being the first son.

Ned received basic schooling, first at Beveridge and later in Avenel, one hundred kilometres north of Melbourne, where the family moved when Ned was nine. It was near Avenel that he once risked his life to save another boy, Richard Shelton, from drowning. As a reward he was given a green sash by the boy's family, which he wore under his armour during the siege in 1880.

The Kellys were suspected many times of cattle or horse stealing, though no conviction was recorded. Red Kelly was eventually arrested when he killed and skinned a calf claimed to be the property of his neighbour. He was found guilty not of cattle theft but of removing the brand from the skin, and given the option of a 25-pound fine or a sentence of six months' imprisonment with hard labour.

Without money to pay the fine, Red spent nearly four months of the sentence in Kilmore Gaol. Two years later, in December 1866, he died of dropsy (oedema – possibly caused by heart or liver disease) at the age of forty-six. Soon afterwards the Kelly family acquired land and moved to the Greta area of north-eastern Victoria, to Eleven Mile Creek where they had family.

The Kellys and their extended family were involved in petty and more serious crimes ranging from assault to theft. At the age of fourteen Ned was convicted of robbing and assaulting a Chinese merchant, Ah Fook. The charges were dropped, but the following year Ned was arrested and accused of being an accomplice to Harry Power, a local bushranger. Again the charges were dropped but historians seem to agree that Ned did range with Power. He was implicated in several more serious crimes, and in 1871 he received a sentence of three years in Pentridge Prison for receiving a stolen horse.

In 2014 I carried out a major excavation at the former Her Majesty's Prison Pentridge in the northern Melbourne suburb of Coburg. The first prison was the 1851–57 Pentridge

Stockade complex, a relatively ad-hoc group of structures built by prison labour and using predominantly local materials. The Stockade was replaced in the late 1850s and early 1860s with the construction of Inspector-General William Champ's model prison complex, based on British exemplars and incorporating a sophisticated system of prisoner classification and penal reform. This complex is where Ned Kelly ended up in 1871.

Champ's prison still sits as a brooding Gothic backdrop at the northern end of Sydney Road, about ten kilometres north of the city of Melbourne. Built of the grey-blue basalt found locally, it resembles a faux medieval castle complete with crenellated battlements, towers, cross-shaped arrow slots (loopholes) and a gate house with a squat Tudor arch. It's very *Game of Thrones*. The location of the prison, its medieval styling and even its proximity to two churches were all deliberate. There is one thing that Victorians (of the time period, not the state) were good at and that was symbolism. When it came to public structures nothing was done by accident.

Since the beginning of the gold rush, the population of Melbourne had exploded and not with an influx of the upstanding middle class. It was swamped with every form of chancer and footloose rainbow-chaser, most of whom failed to make their fortunes. Crime was getting out of hand and the great and the good of Melbourne demanded that something be done. Melbourne Gaol had reached capacity and the prison hulks that rotted at anchor off Williamstown were rat-ridden death traps.

Champ placed his new prison on one of the highest points in north Melbourne. At the time it would have stood on its own, surrounded by farmland, and would have been visible from miles away, including from the city. The strong, impenetrable and familiar design of the prison façade brought comfort to the concerned colonists. Medieval romantic fiction was all the rage and everyone knew that a castle was the epitome of secure lodgings. The menacing image also acted as a deterrent to anyone thinking of taking up a career in crime. The proximity of the churches made the life choice clearer. Either follow the big guy and his teachings or end up in the big house.

As we discovered during the Pentridge dig, the Champ prison was modelled on two systems, the so-called Silent and Separate Systems of incarceration, which had originated in the newly emerged United States of America. One of the things that comes out of a revolution is a burst of energy. Once the dust has settled, the victors have given each other medals and the vanquished have either been pardoned in a chest-swelling example of the magnanimity of the new regime or executed to signal a firm but fair authority. The new society reinvents itself by throwing off the shackles of the old one.

This is what happened after the American War of Independence. Free at last from the burden of the old ways of British colonialism, the Americans set about reinventing everything from money to government. They even started driving on the opposite side of the road. Together with this organisational change came a huge surge in scientific, economic and social thought: an enlightenment. Part of this was a reappraisal of the penal system.

Before independence, approaches to crime and punishment were distinctly British and the British approach was distinctly medieval. Up until the end of the eighteenth century in Britain, if you committed a serious crime such as murder you would be executed, but you could also be hanged for 'being in the company of Gypsies for one month' or 'blacking the face or using a disguise whilst committing a crime' or showing 'strong evidence of malice in a child aged seven to fourteen years' – a heinous crime. At one point, 220 crimes were listed on the British statutes as capital offences, a list which became known as the Bloody Code. Between 1770 and 1830 it was applied 35,000 times, although only 7000 executions were carried out in that time.

The Bloody Code emphasised punishment that saw the possibility of redemption only in the literal presence of God (that is, in death). It also explains why incarceration as a specific punishment was not common until the penal reforms of the early nineteenth century. If your crime sat outside the 220 capital offences you had to pay a fine or suffer being beaten or publicly humiliated, or, if you were lucky, all three. These responses to people who erred against society had been the norm for thousands of years.

But at the beginning of the nineteenth century a push to reform the penal system was gaining momentum in the United

States and elsewhere. The main shift was the belief that there was the possibility of reform and redemption for all but the most serious offenders. The question was what regime could facilitate this. The monastic way of life seemed like a fine example. After all, you didn't see monks filling up the courthouses. When was the last time anyone was mugged by a monk? When did you hear of a monk shoplifting or spraying graffiti or getting into a fight (monks of the Church of the Holy Sepulchre excepted)?

Aspects of monastic life were incorporated into the new model prison system in the United States, with this progressive movement centred on the enormous and extraordinary Eastern State Penitentiary in Philadelphia. Built in 1829, it was the largest and most expensive building in America. Intellectuals and political leaders from all over the world came to marvel at its size, design and the new philosophy that was employed there. The system, known as the Pennsylvania or Separate System, implemented the monastic practice of silent and separate contemplation of one's sins and devotion to God. It required inmates to live in solitary confinement twenty-four hours a day.

Thirty years later, the Separate System was applied to prisoners at Pentridge in the purpose-built A and B Divisions. The design of these prison blocks is very similar to that of Pentonville Prison in North London, which in turn closely follows the Eastern State Penitentiary design.

The Separate System required specific architecture. For instance, each cell (another monastic link – the term cell comes from the architectural name for a monk's sleeping quarters) had a sink and flushing toilet so that the occupant didn't need to leave during the twenty-three hours a day that they were confined. At Eastern State, each cell had access to a small individual exercise yard with walls high enough to exclude visual interaction between inmates. At Pentridge, inmates were exercised for one hour a day, called airing. (I'd imagine after such long confinement the average prisoner would be on the nose, so perhaps airing is a literal term.) Instead of individual exercise yards attached to the cells, at Pentridge sixteen yards were constructed adjacent to the cell blocks around a central watchtower. These 'panopticon' structures, two at B Division and one at A Division, allowed for hundreds of prisoners to be aired each day with only a few prison guards needed to keep the peace.

These are amazing and unique structures. In plan they look like a wagon wheel with the hub being the watchtower. The individual yards radiated out, like the area between spokes, to a circular perimeter. The walls between each yard were of brick, built on rubble foundations of blue basalt. Solitary confinement was maintained throughout. Before the prisoners left their cells they had to place a felt or canvas hood over their head. Eyeholes allowed them to see where they were going but meant they could not communicate via facial expressions during the short walk from their cells to their individual airing yards.

The panopticon design, as applied in Pentridge's adoption of the Separate System, was first proposed by Jeremy Bentham in an essay on penal reform in the 1760s. Bentham is an extraordinary figure of the late eighteenth and early nineteenth centuries. As a philosopher he was the founder of Utilitarianism, a naturalistic moral system which held that the good course of action was that which held the greatest happiness for the greatest number. And if you think that sounds like hippy talk, wait until you hear what else he commented on. As well as being a philosopher, he was a social reformer and jurist and wrote extensively on law and social reforms. He called for the abolition of the death penalty and slavery. He advocated for equal rights for women and gays and freedom of expression. That all this was two hundred or so years ago is quite incredible.

But it was on his ideas for the reformation of the penal system that he directed a substantial number of the estimated thirty million words he wrote during his life. One of his interests was efficiency. And with the panopticon design of the airing yards at Pentridge, sixteen inmates could be observed by one guard. To maintain control, the guard was hidden from the prisoners' view so they could not tell when they were being observed. Severe punishment of any transgression or misbehaviour ensured acquiescence. Once aired, the inmates were trooped back into their cells and the next sixteen would experience the joy of the wind in their hair.

The three panopticon structures of Pentridge were demolished in the early twentieth century and quickly forgotten about until their striking foundations were uncovered during my excavation. Despite the loss of the upper structures, the bluestone wall footings showed clearly the unusual cartwheel plan made by the circular base of the central watch tower and the radiating walls that separated the individual yards. These archaeological remains afforded a rare view of a radical shift in the way society dealt with those on the margins.

The Separate System sounds to our modern ear a draconian and cruel punishment, but at the time it represented a radical social experiment. Life was still very hard in Pentridge but the emphasis was on reform with the possibility of a return to civil society. Nevertheless, there was only so much the gaolers could do; most of the redemption had to come from within, and silence and solitude were seen as the best way of getting a wrong-doer on the right path.

It was not applied, however, for the whole of a prison sentence. Every prisoner, on entering Pentridge, was stripped of their outside clothing, their name and more curiously their crime. None of the guards knew the prisoners' names or why they were behind bars. This could be seen as dehumanising but was intended as a symbolic shedding of a past life and an opportunity to start afresh. Once stripped of their past, every prisoner endured a month for every year of their sentence in the Separate System before graduating to the other regime practised at Pentridge, the Silent System.

When the young ratbag Ned Kelly was sentenced to three years' hard labour at the age of sixteen, he would have spent three months in B Division conforming to the Separate System. While it was a social revolution and the designers meant well, it was a flawed idea. Then as now, a significant percentage of people who ended up in the prison system had mental health issues as well as terrible life experiences. Being forced to fight their demons in silence and isolation often tipped the poor sods over the edge. Bad enough for a hardened criminal, three months in isolation would have been a terrifying ordeal for a sixteen-year-old from the countryside.

It wasn't the effect of the Separate System on the inmates' mental health that consigned it to history. It was the cost and the increased demand for prison accommodation as Victoria's population exploded in the second half of the nineteenth century. Prisons like Pentridge became too expensive to build, so by the beginning of the twentieth century, two prisoners were being accommodated in the cells and they remained dual occupancy until the prison was closed in 1997.

The parallel system used at Pentridge, the Silent System, was also developed in the north-eastern United States, where it was known as the Auburn or New York System. It was developed at Auburn Prison in New York at about the same time as the Separate System and also used at the famous Sing Sing Prison just to the north of Manhattan. It employed another monastic, penitential regime: that of hard labour.

The largest archaeological trench we excavated was in the middle of Pentridge and uncovered the surface features and sub-surface foundations of C Division, where the Silent System operated. Called the prison within a prison, it was isolated by a high perimeter wall. Inside, six double-storey blocks housed over 360 prisoners in tiny cells. They were so small that there was nowhere to stand when the bed roll was laid out, so during the day the mattress and bedding were rolled into a corner. Unlike the cells in A and B divisions, there was no light, natural or otherwise. There was no heating or cooling, of course, ventilation was minimal and there was no loo. Just a bucket to keep your nose company on those long summer nights ... it must have been a miserable place. In the 1880s, a governmental inspection of prisons concluded that C Division was unfit for human habitation and should be demolished. Clearly the Pentridge management took this report on board and did demolish C Division. They just waited ninety years first. It remained in use, unmodified, until the 1970s. One of the old guards who came to visit the dig told me that the smell of C Division was unbelievable.

'It's a smell that will never leave me,' he said. 'It was a mixture of excrement, urine and unwashed bodies.'

But while the accommodation was much worse for the young Ned Kelly after he graduated from B Division, at least he could rub shoulders with his fellow inmates. He just wasn't allowed to speak to them. (It wasn't called the Silent System for nothing.) The Silent System revolved around work, thirteen hours a day, every day of the year. In the early days it was menial tasks such as breaking rocks, but quickly the industries attached to the prison expanded and became comprehensive and profitable.

Prisoners made everything for the prison from uniforms to yard brooms. They made tools and equipment for the local council and colonial government. We found a large cast-iron book press on site suggesting that more highly skilled tasks were performed. Even the press itself was cast in the prison foundry.

Once more you can look on the Silent System as harsh punishment. But at that time most people worked long hours and six-day weeks, so the level of work wasn't out of the ordinary. For many of the inmates this regime may have been the first time that they had been taught anything or gained a skill, and perhaps a feeling of self-worth.

The excavation uncovered the startling ruins of buildings that represented an extraordinary shift in the way society dealt with people on the margins. It showed a colony able to undertake significant public works of cutting-edge design and implement progressive social programs. It was still, however, the nineteenth century, and there was a fair share of fatal beatings, cruelty and terrible hardships.

There is little doubt that the young Ned Kelly went into Pentridge as a cocky larrikin and came out a hardened, bitter and angry man.

*

Once out of prison, Ned worked at a variety of jobs, including shaping sleepers for the railway to Beechworth, and it's perhaps his knowledge of railway construction that gave him the idea to later derail the police train at Glenrowan.

In 1877 Ned gave up any pretence of traditional work and embarked full-time on horse stealing and gold prospecting. With his friends and younger brother, he established a lucrative horse-stealing business in the north-east of Victoria and along the New South Wales border. It's likely that that would have been the extent of the gang's activities but for a fateful encounter.

On 15 April 1878, local police constable Alexander Fitzpatrick was shot in the wrist at the Kelly homestead while attempting to arrest Dan Kelly for theft. Whether the wounding of Fitzpatrick was an accident, a provoked incident or a malicious attack, Ned Kelly and his brother and close friends became marked men. Arrest warrants were issued for Dan and Ned for attempted murder.

The brothers took to the bush, leaving their mother, Ellen, to face the courts. She was sentenced to three years in Pentridge Prison for aiding and abetting the attempted murder of Fitzpatrick.

The boys retreated to the Wombat Ranges, north of Mansfield in Victoria, and spent the winter gold prospecting and distilling illicit whisky. But their bush camp was soon discovered. On 25 October 1878, Sergeant Kennedy set off from Mansfield to the Wombat Ranges to search for the Kelly brothers, accompanied by Constables McIntyre, Lonigan and Scanlon. The police set up a camp near two shepherd huts at Stringybark Creek in a heavily timbered area. A second police party had set off from Greta with the intention of closing in on the gang in a pincer movement.

On arrival at Stringybark Creek, Kennedy's team split into two. Kennedy and Scanlon went in search of the gang, while Lonigan and McIntyre remained to set up the camp. Unaware they were only a mile away from the Kelly camp, Lonigan and McIntyre took pot shots at parrots. Alerted by the shooting, the gang discovered the police camp and decided to overpower the two officers, then wait for the two others to return.

Ned and Dan approached the police camp and ordered the police officers to surrender. Constable McIntyre threw his arms up but Lonigan went for his revolver and Ned shot him. Mortally wounded, Lonigan staggered into the bush and died. When the other two police returned to camp, Constable McIntyre, at Ned's direction, called on them to surrender. Scanlon went for his pistol and Ned fired and shot him dead. Kennedy ran, firing as he sought cover. In an exchange of gunfire, Kennedy was shot and wounded, possibly fatally. Ned then questioned the unarmed Kennedy for two hours before shooting him at point-blank range through the heart. McIntyre, in the confusion, escaped on horseback uninjured. Leaving the camp, Ned took Sergeant Kennedy's handwritten note for his wife and his gold fob watch. Asked later why he stole the watch, Ned replied, 'What's the use of a watch to a dead man?'

The Victorian parliament passed the Felons' Apprehension Act in response to the slaying of the three police officers. The act outlawed the gang and legitimised a general shoot-to-kill policy on the four gang members.

Despite an extensive and aggressive police search, the Kellys, Joe Byrne and Steve Hart remained at large for twenty months. In that time they committed two major robberies, at Euroa in Victoria and Jerilderie in New South Wales. This period on the run was described as the 'Kelly Outrage' by the popular press, and their notoriety spread across Australia and to Britain. Responding to an exasperated public and criticism from the colonial rulers both in Victoria and London, the police redoubled their efforts to track down the outlaws but with little success.

Perhaps emboldened by his gang's seeming invincibility and flattered by the media and public attention, together with guilt for the privations caused to their family and friends by constant police attention, Ned Kelly decided to bring matters to a head and strike a decisive blow against the authorities. He planned to lure a special police train to the area, derail it and ambush the occupants at Glenrowan. Some historians have suggested that this was part of a coordinated revolution to establish a republic.

The gang suspected that Aaron Sherritt, Joe Byrne's best friend and sometime gang member, was a police informant. Ned Kelly decided that his murder would be sufficient to bring a train load of police to the area and at the same time provide a strong example to others who may have thought to betray the gang for the considerable bounty offered by the authorities.

On 26 June 1880, Dan Kelly and Joe Byrne went to Sherritt's house near Beechworth, approximately forty kilometres to the east of Glenrowan, and shot him dead in front of his wife and mother-in-law. Four policemen who were staying with him at the time hid under the bed and did not report the murder until late the following morning. Either these guys were the Keystone Cops or the gang's reputation was even more fearsome than I had appreciated. This delay was to prove crucial since it upset Ned's timing for the main ambush.

Meanwhile, Steve Hart and Ned Kelly travelled to Glenrowan, arriving late on the same Saturday night at McDonnell's Hotel, located on the opposite side of the tracks to Ann Jones's Glenrowan Inn. From there they travelled approximately eight hundred metres down the line north-east of the Glenrowan station, where they attempted to rip up a section of rail. At this point the train, coming from Melbourne, would have passed through Glenrowan and be accelerating down from the Glenrowan Pass into the Ovens Valley as it headed towards Wangaratta and Beechworth, the closest station to Sherritt's house. A lifted rail would flip the train down an embankment twenty metres into a creek. There is no doubt that the train wreck would have killed or maimed all aboard.

Ned's iconic armour, fashioned from plough mould boards, was not designed, as is often assumed, to protect the wearer in a face-to-face gun battle, but to protect the wearer while he picked off any survivors of the train wreck. It's also thought that the armour was intended to be a striking, if contrived, image of knights on a noble quest (Ned Kelly was thought to have been a fan of *Lorna Doone* and Walter Scott's *Ivanhoe* – both of which depicted knights in armour and had strong themes of standing up to authority and fighting for the downtrodden).

The plan began to further unravel, however, when Steve and Ned were unable to lift the rail by themselves. They walked back into Glenrowan late on the Saturday night and headed towards what they thought was a rail workers' camp on the northern edge of the rail reserve. Ned woke the foreman, a guy called Piazzi, and a scuffle broke out and a shot was fired. Piazzi wasn't alone in his tent and was not happy that his amorous evening had been disturbed.

It turned out that the men were gravel contractors who had been billeted in Glenrowan for months to haul gravel to the rail for transport to Benalla, where the rock was being used to lay out the main streets, and they did not have the right tools to break the rail.

Up to this point the Kelly Gang had no intention of involving the Glenrowan township in the ambush and no plan to take hostages. But to ensure the proposed ambush remained secret, Ned had to detain the gravel workers. Ned and Steve took the workers to the Glenrowan Inn, less than a hundred metres to the west of the campsite. Perhaps fearful that the shot had woken Ann Jones and her family, Steve Hart took them hostage also, while Ned raised some real railway workers and got them to work on breaking the rail. These workers too were then taken hostage.

The police response to Sherritt's murder was slow, and by the time the special train (there were no services on Sunday) neared Glenrowan, thirty-three hours had elapsed. Over this period, Dan and Joe had ridden to the inn and more members of the Glenrowan community were taken hostage, until sixty-two people were being held at the inn.

The delay took its toll on the gang. Lack of sleep and food and perhaps too much alcohol may have contributed to a fatal mistake made by Ned in allowing the Glenrowan teacher Thomas Curnow to leave the inn unescorted just hours before the police train arrived. Curnow had pleaded with Ned to let him go home to his sick wife. He had promised not to alert anyone of the plan or the gang's presence in the town, and Ned had believed him. Curnow followed the track towards Melbourne and stopped the train about 1.5 kilometres short of the town, briefing the police on the situation at the inn. The gang only knew that their plan had failed when they heard the train stop at the station instead of rattling through.

Hastily, the four gang members fitted their armour and moved out onto the verandah to face the approaching police party. At three o'clock in the morning on 28 June, the siege commenced with an initial volley fired by the gang and returned by the police, who formed positions in the creek that ran to the south and south-east of the inn.

While their armour provided some protection, Ned Kelly and Joe Byrne were wounded in the first volley – Ned seriously. A bullet passed through both the forearm and bicep of his bent arm. Another bullet seriously damaged his right thumb, and as the gang retreated into the inn, Ned was shot in the heel.

The timber walls provided little protection, and the projectiles from the Martini-Henry rifles (the standard colonial-issue rifle at the time) and other assorted weapons of the police ripped through the walls. All the terrified hostages could do was lie on the floor. Outside, someone called, 'Don't fire. The place is full of women and children, stop firing.' In groups, the hostages were released, but not before Martin Cherry, a local, was mortally wounded and Ann Jones's son, John (Jack) Jones was shot. He died later in Wangaratta.

Jack Lloyd, Ned's cousin and a leading Kelly sympathiser, was waiting in front of McDonnell's Hotel to launch two Chinese rockets once the train was derailed. This was to be the signal to sympathisers to ride to Glenrowan and join the gang. From there they were to ride to Benalla and hold up the Bank of New South Wales and declare the 'Republic of North-East Victoria'. It is likely that Jack panicked on hearing the exchange of fire, or perhaps it was a call to arms, but either way he let off the rockets. The number of sympathisers is not known, with accounts describing between thirty and 150 gathering to the north-east of the inn. Ned left the inn and warned the sympathisers to stay out of the battle, although there is no evidence that any meeting with the group took place.

Ned returned undetected to the inn at approximately 4.30am. As he entered the bar room, Joe Byrne stood at the counter and, raising a whisky, toasted to 'many more years in the bush for the Kelly Gang'. At that moment a volley of fire ripped through the front wall of the inn and Joe took a bullet in the groin and quickly bled to death.

With his best friend gone, Ned resolved to escape under cover of darkness, but for some reason Steve and Dan did not follow, and Ned found himself to the north-east of the battle, alone. Some accounts say that he passed out from loss of blood at this stage. If so, he came to and advanced on the police lines from the northeast at first light. The surprise attack has gone down in history; the image of Kelly in armour and a full-length greatcoat firing his archaic pistols and taking shot after shot before collapsing from leg wounds is now legendary. Ned was captured and some twenty-eight wounds on him were tended at the railway station.

The siege of the inn continued throughout the day and, fearful that the remaining gang members might escape during the approaching winter evening, the police decided to set fire to the building and flush them out. Hay and oil were placed against the western wall and set alight. Before the fuel began to burn too furiously, a priest and a police officer entered the pub and retrieved Joe Byrnes's body. During a quick search of the rest of the inn they observed Dan Kelly and Steve Hart lying arm in arm, dead, in the western bedroom. Whether they had committed suicide or died from wounds sustained in the long gunfight is not known. Their bodies could not be retrieved before the fire took hold of the room and when their burned corpses were recovered once the fire was out, they were immediately handed over to the Kelly family and friends, who had witnessed the siege.

The siege was over. Ann Jones had lost her son, her business, her stock and her house. Another hostage, Martin Cherry, had died and others were wounded or emotionally scarred. Dan Kelly, Steve Hart and Joe Byrne were dead and Ned Kelly was not expected to live. He did, however, and was transported to Melbourne. Five months later he stood trial for the murder of Constable Lonigan at Stringybark Creek.

Despite some vocal public support and a frenzied press, Kelly was found guilty and hanged on 11 November 1880 at Melbourne Gaol – the place of execution until 1921, when the gaol was closed and the gallows were transferred to Pentridge.

*

Once I knew what had happened, the most important question for me was to identify from the records what had survived from that brief gun battle of 128 years before. Fortunately, a detailed account of the inn was given during the royal commission into the siege. This would help us determine where to dig; in addition it gave me an understanding of what had been there at the time and what was likely to have survived. Knowing the layout of the building, I could appreciate the challenges faced by the gang: the access and the protection (or lack of) afforded by the building materials. These were details of the practicalities of the siege often overlooked by historical accounts but important to the success of the dig.

In 1878 Ann Jones had commissioned local builders, Messrs Emery and Jarvis from Wangaratta, to construct an inn on her land immediately to the south of her house. The original plan was for a three-room single-gabled building, but Ann Jones requested that two bedrooms be added with a skillion-roofed lean-to. Costing two hundred pounds, the inn was constructed of weatherboards painted white and had an iron roof, also painted white. At the time the inn was claimed to be better than McDonnell's Hotel, being larger, with a better bar counter and floorboards as opposed to earthen floors. Evidence given at the royal commission following the siege explained that the inn was doing well and the persons patronising the inn were working class.

The frame of the inn – the wall studs, wall plates, bearers, joists, rafters, battens and ceiling joists – was sawn timber. These were joined with handmade square-head nails. Flooring would have been abutting pine boards approximately three centimetres thick. Vertical frame posts would have been set into post holes but the floor bearers and wall base plates may have sat on floor joists which in turn sat directly on the ground.

The doors were panelled and possibly imported from the United States, and the parlour door was part-glazed with coloured glass panels (most likely paper transfer rather than lead light). The chimneys were locally made terracotta-coloured brick, while the internal fireplaces were rendered up to a chest-high timber mantle.

The walls and ceilings were lined with stretched hessian, which would have been painted. The skirting would have been twenty-five centimetres of red pine (Californian redwood) and it is likely that the three main public rooms would have had pine dado panelling. The windows were double hung with square glass panels.

Analysis of photographic evidence showed that the inn measured approximately nine metres wide by four metres to the rear of the main gabled structure with an additional three metres to the north incorporating the lean-to bedrooms.

The southern wall, facing the rail reserve and taking the brunt of the police fire, had two doorways – one into the bar and one into the dining room – and three windows, one each for the parlour at the west, the bar in the middle and the dining room to the east. These openings would have been the only locations that the Kelly Gang could shoot from.

A verandah ran along the southern wall with its roof supported by six timber posts. The main gabled portion of the inn had brick fireplaces and chimneys at the east and west end. Less is known of the northern wall as there are no photos or drawings of the inn from the north. We do know, however, that a single door behind the bar gave access to a short hallway between the two bedrooms. A rear door at the end of the hallway opened onto a narrow 'breezeway' between the inn and Ann Jones's residence and allowed access between the kitchen – which was in the residence – and the dining room in the inn.

The torching of the inn to end the siege completely destroyed the building. The brick chimneys survived, and up against the western chimney Ann built a modest hut as a temporary home until compensation for her losses was agreed on and paid. She had to wait eighteen months until after the royal commission into the siege had been concluded.

With the 265 pounds Ann received in compensation, she commissioned another building. It was a large weatherboard house on what was now a corner block. But Ann was unable to regain her liquor licence so, ironically, she leased the building to the Victorian police. Very little is known about this second building and there is only one photograph of it. However, it appears to have occupied an area slightly larger than the original inn, and extended further to the north. It is also likely during the time between its construction in 1882 and 1902, when it burned down, additional outbuildings were constructed to the rear. The location and function of these structures is not recorded. The police occupied the building until 1895 when a new police house to the east along Siege Street was completed. Ann Jones reoccupied the house at that time. Sometime before 1902 a liquor licence was given and the thirteen-room building became a wine shop and hotel. Ann Jones (who had remarried and was then known as Ann Smith) moved away, leasing the wine shop and hotel business until it was destroyed by fire.

After the fire, the land remained vacant for a while, and sometime prior to the First World War a third and final building was constructed on the site. This time the building was brick and built on a similar floor plan to the second timber wine shop. It was also run as a wine shop (locally known as a wine shanty) called the Café Royal and had a common room, dining room, parlour and bedrooms.

In the early 1940s it was renamed the Last Stand Café. Photos show the building with a hipped tin roof and splayed corner entrance and a bull-nosed verandah. Over the years it functioned as a café, wine shanty, guesthouse, confectionary and drink shop and hair salon.

The site was cleared in 1976–77 by the present landowner and the land has remained vacant since then.

The description of the original inn and subsequent buildings was remarkably comprehensive and provided me with a good understanding of the land's history. The trouble was, so much had happened on the site since the events in 1880 that it was possible nothing survived of the original inn, never mind evidence of such a brief event as the siege. Uncertainties such as this are commonplace in archaeology but the considerable expectation, excitement and media attention surrounding the excavation added to the normal stresses of preparing for a dig.

I needn't have worried. I gathered together the best team of archaeologists in the country and, over a period of four weeks, we discovered incredibly well-preserved evidence of this most famous gunfight.

The archaeology was complex, and so were other aspects of the dig. Across the rail tracks from the site is the Glenrowan Hotel, now the only pub in town. We often had a few drinks out on the front verandah after work. The night before we started the dig, I had gathered the team together and warned them not to give their personal opinions about the Kelly Gang in the pub or around the town. 'We are here to do a job. As professional archaeologists we need to be, and perhaps more importantly be seen to be, as objective and impartial as possible.'

The team were great and we maintained a good relationship with the Glenrowan community throughout the project – or most of them. About a week into the dig I drove past the pub and noticed a huge pile of horse manure dumped on the verandah where we had been the night before. I stopped the car and stared. It would have to have been a large trailer load, gently steaming in the morning sun and partly covering the chairs and tables.

Our attempts at winning the hearts and minds of the locals clearly still had some way to go. But then it could have been worse. They could have dumped the manure on us.

Part of the public engagement program provided an opportunity for members of the public to come and dig on the site for a couple of hours. There were thousands of expressions of interest for about a dozen places. Thus is the popularity of Ned Kelly. Those who see him as a folk hero are very passionate about their belief and have the t-shirts, bumper stickers, books and fake armour to prove it. One such fan got an opportunity to dig on the site.

I looked up at the intense face as my hand was slightly crushed in his gloved hand, briefly questioning whether the volunteer program had been a good idea. He was clearly a fan of Ned Kelly and was really excited to be allowed on site. I set him to work with a trowel and asked him to scrape a section to the rear of the inn foundations where the bedrooms had been.

A while later I looked up and saw a bit of commotion among the volunteers. I walked over to find my muscular friend holding a lead projectile in his hand.

'Is this a bullet?' he asked me.

I looked at it carefully and said, 'Yep, that's likely to have come from one of the police rifles during the siege.'

'Really?'

'Yep.'

He burst into tears.

If that reaction didn't demonstrate the emotion tied up in this dig enough, another incident showed just how close to home it was. Halfway through the dig, I was giving a talk to the local primary school kids. After standing patiently while I spouted on about what we were doing and what we had found so far, one lad at the end put up his hand.

'Yes?' I said.

He puffed out his chest a little and said, 'Ned Kelly's sister is my great-grandmother.'

I heard the trowelling stop and saw that my team were all staring at the young lad. This was a unique experience for an archaeologist; there is usually a disconnect between the lives that we are excavating and those in the here and now. For most of my career I have tried to bridge that gap and bring the stories of the past into the present. This dig was different. *This* past was still directly connected to the community and we were nosing around in other people's business. I have never felt such a great responsibility to get an excavation right.

After the dig was done, we returned to film a TV documentary (more on that later). Over ten days we carried out extra investigations into sections of the inn that we hadn't had time to complete during the original dig. We also got a chance to have a bit of fun doing some experimental archaeology.

During the original dig we had assumed that a line of squashed lead projectiles represented bullets that had smashed through the front wall of the timber inn building coming to rest along the base of the rear wall that had halted their violent progress through the building. This assumption seemed entirely reasonable but with no timber relics we didn't have any proof. We also assumed that melted glass fragments recovered from the site were the result of an unusually fierce fire caused by the large amounts of flammable liquor Ann Jones had stored in the pub. But again we didn't have any proof.

For the documentary we decided to test these assumptions by building a section of the inn, then shooting at it and burning it to the ground with a load of booze inside. I roped in my father-in-law, Graeme, and brother-in-law, Matt, to build a section of timber wall in a manner typical of building construction in the late nineteenth century and then carted it to a firing range.

Sure enough, the lead flew through the timber walls, spraying splinters in all directions, and showed in a very dramatic way what a terrifying place those three front rooms would have been during the siege. When we set fire to our construction with about two dozen bottles of cheap brandy inside, we were taken aback by the ferocity of the blaze that shattered the bottles like small bombs and consumed the structure in seconds.

It was enormous fun to do and useful for the analysis of the archaeological evidence, but very sobering as well. This wasn't some abstract history lesson. This was archaeology up close and personal.

Unexpectedly, near the end of the documentary shoot, we discovered a group of copper percussion caps and cartridges in a corner where the rear bedroom once stood. This was an extremely exciting and important find, as they could only have been dropped by members of the Kelly Gang. Henry Huggins is a retired forensic officer who used to work with the Victorian police. His expertise was comparative analysis of ballistics, essentially matching bullets to guns. I had employed Henry to look at the munitions discovered during the dig and I got him back to be involved in the documentary.

I showed him the percussion caps and other cartridges. 'Do you think you can match any of these to the Kelly Gang's weapons?' I asked.

'Sure, if you can get me the guns,' Henry shrugged.

Historical accounts of the gang's weapons described a mixture of pistols, rifles and shotguns. If we were going to find a match, we had a better chance of isolating Ned's from the others because for some reason Ned preferred to use old-fashioned guns that were muzzle-loaded and used tiny match-head-sized percussion caps. We also knew that a man called Rupert Hammond in Canberra claimed to own Ned's archaic Colt revolving carbine. It had been passed down through his family but its provenance had never been verified.

We invited Rupert to bring the old gun down so that we could prove once and for all whether the weapon he owned was Ned's, and also to see if these tiny percussion caps were discarded by the man himself. Under glaring lights and with a roomful of film crew and excited archaeologists, Henry Huggins methodically analysed a distinctive crescent-shaped crease on the old percussion cap with a piece of foil marked by the hammer action of the weapon owned by Rupert.

We waited.

Henry squinted through the microscope and then with no fanfare, he said, 'They're a match.'

It was an amazing moment. The smallest artefact we had found was a definite link to the legend. Also, with that percussion cap we could for the first time map the movements of the boys in their final hours. This corner of the rear room must have been the safest place for the gang to reload, because the front rooms were clearly no place to hang around in. It was one of those moments when you pause and think about what you have discovered.

The charred timbers, melted glass and squashed lead represented moments of terror and menace that affected the survivors forever and left five people dead. The small cluster of percussion caps and cartridges in the back room spoke less of a courageous fight against authority than a sad and frantic scrap for survival after an ambitious plan gone wrong.

One forgets that legends, while romantic in their telling, are often based on tragedy. It took an archaeological dig to bring the Ned Kelly story back to reality.

OF TV, TALES AND TURKEY SHOOTS

The past, present and future walked into a bar. It was tense.

Anonymous (I'll get my coat)

A loud sniff at the bedroom door was followed by a deep, throaty and supremely menacing growl. It was a growl that started in the bowels and shoulder-barged its way to a rough and angry throat. It was a growl that could only come from a mouth full of sharp fangs that dripped fetid saliva. It was a growl that immediately preceded extreme violence, and it was a growl that had my undivided attention as I sat on the edge of a strange bed, in a huge old empty house, in the dark, filming myself with a small night-vision camera.

This was a situation that on the face of it was distinctly weird and kinky.

*

I'd first become involved in film in 2006, when I made two short documentaries with a local production team while excavating a site in Bendigo. I liked the idea of relating the story of a dig in a way that would engage people. Then, shortly before the Kelly Gang dig, three guys from the local TV news crew in the New South Wales–Victoria border town of Albury contacted me and asked if they could film it. They were great guys who had decided to take a month's leave without pay to record the excavation in the hope of perhaps cutting it into a documentary.

I didn't have a problem with that, but what I didn't appreciate was that they would be there every day. It fell mostly to me, as the dig director, to talk on camera. I rather enjoyed this. I had long been a fan of the UK archaeology TV show *Time Team*, and I admired the way the presenter, Tony Robinson, broke through the dry and dusty archaeological data to tell the fascinating stories of the past. I was no Tony Robinson, but I felt a responsibility to tell the remarkable episode of the siege and what we were learning from the dig. Little did I know that a few months later I'd be working with Tony.

The film crew were certainly dedicated, and I think this archaeological project is, to date, the most extensively filmed dig in Australian history. Somewhere there is also a bloopers reel that I fervently hope will never see the light of day ...

In fact, when I first heard that I had got the Kelly dig, I called a good friend of mine, Alex West. He's an award-winning filmmaker who in a previous life was an archaeologist, and we had already talked about making a documentary based around an archaeological excavation. 'Alex, you know as well as I do that this is the only time this site is going to be excavated, and you don't get any bigger than digging up the Kelly legend. We have to film it.'

He agreed, and over the next couple of months worked hard to put together a pitch to persuade the ABC to make the film. He was successful, but the national broadcaster's rigorous nature of accountability and value for money means that it is sometimes not the quickest ship to get moving, so by the time the funding was approved and contracting was completed, the excavation was over. If it hadn't been for the great work and thorough film coverage by the Albury guys, the documentary would not have been made.

With their raw footage, we were able to go back to the site later in 2006 and uncover it again. We spent two weeks filming additional material to shape up the documentary that became *Ned Kelly Uncovered*. When the film crew had first contemplated losing a month's pay to film a dig in the middle of winter, they had joked that it would be worth it if they could get Tony Robinson to present it. Years before, Alex had directed a couple of *Time Team* eposides, and with his connections realised their dream. You should have seen their faces when they met Tony in Glenrowan the night before he started shooting their film.

To be honest, I was as awestruck as they were. I wasn't only a big fan of *Time Team*, I had also grown up rolling around the floor laughing at the fabulous *Blackadder* comedy series, and I'd particularly loved Tony Robinson's character, Baldrick. So when I met him for the first time, it took great self-control not to quote *Blackadder* lines at him. I had a feeling that he'd probably heard them all before and had said them with much better comedic timing.

The documentary turned out to be fun to make and a great film, but it was also a turning point in my career.

*

By the time I had completed the Kelly dig, the archaeological excavation report and the ABC documentary I was exhausted. For the previous five or so years, I had been juggling five to eight projects at a time, as well as building a business and trying (and generally failing) to be the husband and father that the girls deserved and that I wanted to be. I felt like I had to take a break from the job for a while. I was feeling stale as well as wiped out, and I knew it was time to do something else. I needed a complete change.

I wasn't sure what, though. Maybe we could take the girls out of school and travel round Europe for a year? Or maybe I could write? Perhaps we could go and live in the UK for a while? My mum and dad were elderly and I missed them, along with my brothers and sister and their families. Also, it would be great to reconnect with all my old friends from school and university. And, despite all the challenges of the great British weather, I missed that nutty nation off to the left of Europe collectively called the United Kingdom of Great Britain and Northern Ireland, which I still think includes some of the most beautiful islands in the world.

And then my mother died. I came back from the UK after the funeral tired and sad and changed, as one is by these events. At the risk of sounding trite, I had returned with a clear understanding of the finite nature of our lives and the need to seize the day. I was determined more than ever that I was not going to be grinding away at stuff I wasn't particularly interested in doing. But I did not want to make any decision about our future while still reeling from grief, so we were undecided five months later when I got a phone call out of the blue from a TV producer called Daniel Brown.

He'd seen the Ned Kelly documentary and wondered if I would be interested working on a TV series he was developing. I said, 'Sure,' and we arranged to meet in Melbourne. When I told Inga, she asked what the job was. I realised I hadn't found out. She walked off, shaking her head. I'd just assumed that he wanted me to be the archaeology boffin. Walk on, say something archaeological, walk off.

When we met, I asked what I was to do.

He looked at me as if I was stupid. 'We want you to present it.'

'Why?' I blurted back. In the back of my mind I thought, *What did you say that for? Just say yes, you fool!*

He looked a bit taken aback. 'Well, it's going to be an archaeology, history-type show, and we want a presenter who is an archaeologist. And you are the only archaeologist we know of who's done some TV.'

'Oh. Okay then.'

That's how I ended up sitting in the dark with the Hound of the Baskervilles slavering at the door. I was in a massive old house near Perth Airport, and I was filming the last episode of the first series of the ABC TV show *Who's Been Sleeping in My House?* It was about three o'clock in the morning. The film crew had left four hours before, and I was staying in the supposedly haunted house on my own to see if I could feel anything supernatural. I hadn't had the heart to tell the director that I didn't believe in ghosts, and clearly she hadn't had the heart to tell me that they were leaving behind the homeowner's eighty-kilo Rottweiler called Cujo (no, really).

For those who haven't seen the show – and look, that's okay – I travel to old houses around Australia and investigate the stories of the people who've lived in them. *Who's Been Sleeping in My House?* was Dan's brainchild. He had just sold his house in Perth and realised that the purchaser was going to knock it down to build a bunch of townhouses. It wasn't a particularly notable building and wasn't especially old, perhaps interwar. But it held special memories because he had started a family there, and it had rung with the giggles and ruckus of little people doing what little people do. He decided its history needed celebrating somehow before it fell to the wrecking ball, so he traced as many previous owners as he could and invited them to a farewell barbecue in the back yard.

Standing around the sausages with a few cold beers in the Perth afternoon sun, Dan was amazed at the stories delivered with such emotion by the previous owners. This unremarkable house had certainly left a remarkable legacy in the memories and feelings of the people who had called it home. The germ of an idea was sown and soon we were talking on the phone, developing a possible show.

Developing a show. If you say it quickly, it sounds quite easy. It's not. At this stage we didn't have a title, but Dan was clear that it was to be an excursion into the past history of houses to find out who had lived there. Eventually, he came up with the title *Who's Been Sleeping in My House?* and from there the show gained sufficient momentum for the ABC to agree to fund a pilot episode.

Dan, who was originally from the UK, had lived and worked in Perth, Western Australia, for about ten years, but like me he had grown up watching UK history shows and wanted to create something similar in Australia.

The pilot was shot at a house in Coolgardie, a small town about six hours' drive east of Perth and only twenty minutes from its more well-known neighbour, Kalgoorlie, in the central goldfields of Western Australia. I remember saying goodbye to Inga as I left for the airport and asking her what the hell I was doing. She smiled at me and said, 'Something different.'

Up to this point everything had seemed quite abstract. All the meetings, apart from the first, had been via Skype or on the phone. I was flattered to be asked to present the series, even though I secretly thought they were stark staring mad. I had limited experience in front of the camera and none at all in presenting a television program. But I had given numerous radio interviews and I'd made a reasonable fist of the *Ned Kelly Uncovered* shoots. I'd also been fortunate enough to work on one of the hugely popular *Time Team* episodes the summer before, and that was another story …

*

As I was saying goodbye to Tony Robinson at the end of the Kelly documentary shoot, he said, 'Well, I've been on one of your digs. When you're back in the UK you need to come on one of mine. Just give me a bell.'

Six months later I trundled up a muddy track and parked next to a massive white marquee that was surrounded by porta-cabins, smaller tents and lots of people moving purposefully with walkie-talkies and clipboards.

I stood for a moment, trying to work out where to go, then I heard someone calling my name and turned around to see Tony rushing up.

He gave me a big hug. 'I'm so sorry to hear about your mum.' It was less than three months since she had died and these simple comforting words meant a great deal. I nodded my thanks and we stomped off to find one of the producers.

I was at a place called Dinmore Hill in Herefordshire and we were an hour from starting a *Time Team* shoot. *Time Team* ran for twenty years, airing its last episode in 2013. Each episode charted an archaeological dig carried out over a three-day timeframe. Tony presented the show and explained the intricacies and technical aspects in layman's terms. The show featured over 270 excavations and popularised archaeology in Britain and around the world.

The site at Dinmore Hill turned out to be an Iron Age promontory enclosure, a wide open hilltop protected by an enormous ditch and bank. It was probably ceremonial. (Just between you and me, if you hear archaeologists describing an archaeological site as ceremonial, it means they don't have a clue what it is.)

Time Team showed all the aspects of field archaeology, including digging and survey techniques, as well as the challenges, wild theories, disappointments and, of course, the archaeological discoveries that are part and parcel of a dig. I've heard criticisms that the frenetic nature of the three-day time limit doesn't reflect real-world archaeology, but I could never see what the fuss was about. The show's team never claimed that they were going to fully dig a site in three days. They would just answer some basic questions. Namely, is there any archaeology there, what is it, how old is it and what happened to it?

I've conducted many test excavations of similar duration with the aim of answering the same questions. But my digs didn't have the great catering van.

*

I'd enjoyed the mental challenge of developing the show with Dan, but standing in the garden of the house in Coolgardie, watching the team set up the camera and sound gear, I felt terrified. Looking back with the experience I have now, I appreciate just how difficult the shoot was. I was learning how to present and the team were figuring out how to put the show together.

Then in the days leading up to the broadcast of the first episode, more terror: it suddenly occurred to me that everyone I knew and possibly hundreds of thousands of others were going to see me on TV. I felt like someone had poured ice-cold water over me. What if I was embarrassingly bad? I started to panic. This could be worse than when I crapped myself in front of everyone in Syria. So it was a huge relief when the pilot – which became the first episode – was well received by the ABC, TV reviewers and the people at home.

I've filmed twenty episodes now, mostly with the same crew, so we are all good friends and the shoots are a lot of fun. Even though we now know what we are doing, shoots are surprisingly complex, and occasionally a scene or a linking piece of dialogue or shot is missed and a reshoot is needed to complete the program.

There was one instance when an omission in the raw film wasn't noticed for a while, which made the reshoot a bit tricky.

I had just sat down with a weary grunt after a long hot day on a dig in central Turkey. I had the mouth of a beautifully chilled bottle of Efes beer at my lips when I was surprised by my phone giving a little buzz. I frowned. I hadn't had any contact with the outside world in days and was convinced the Turkish SIM I had bought in Istanbul had been disabled by the powers that be. You are as free as a bird to purchase a SIM card and even a phone in Turkey, but if you are a foreign national, you have to register said communications purchase at the government tax office or your phone will be cut off within a month. I didn't know this and hadn't done so before moving to the middle of nowhere.

I looked at the email. I read it again and then a third time with the screen held increasingly further away. It seemed my eyesight had deteriorated during the excavation. But the main reason I had to go over it a couple of times was I didn't believe what I was reading. The email was from the production team back in Perth. They needed some extra scenes filmed and would I be able to get to Istanbul for a couple of days at the end of July, in two weeks' time? The unbelievable bit was a request to find a couple of outdoor locations that looked like Sydney and one, if possible, that looked like Sydney Harbour.

I didn't know Istanbul very well, as I'd only stayed there for three days. But there was one thing I knew with absolute certainty: it was not remotely like Sydney.

Dave, the cameraman who had shot the whole of the second series, had been filming for twenty-seven days straight at the London Olympic Games, so when he arrived at a bar in Istanbul's historic district of Sultanahmet he looked shattered. He downed a cold beer, squinted up at the glorious summer evening and then at me.

I was exhausted too. The dig had been on the edge of a little village, Hayiroglu, an hour to the south-east of Konya, slap-bang in the middle of the Konya Plateau. Even though the site sits at a thousand metres above sea level, it is very hot in the summer, and we had been digging for four weeks in temperatures above forty degrees.

Dave did a double-take and burst out laughing. 'This isn't going to work, you've got a tan!' he said.

'You're telling me. I've been digging in the middle of nowhere in this heat for a month.'

'Well, I brought some powder. Maybe we can make you pasty again.'

'Thanks, but the bigger problem is how are we going to disguise the fact that we are in Istanbul and not Sydney?'

He shrugged.

The next day we arrived at the American School of Ottoman Studies, which had given us permission to use its library to shoot some internal scenes. This worked out fine, and by the end of the day we had shot all the linking scenes, and even a couple of street scenes as the surrounding laneways to the American School bore a passing resemblance to Paddington. Well, if you didn't look too closely. It was the last request that was going to be a problem. The editors wanted a final piece to camera to wrap up the episode and they wanted it to be shot with a view that looked like Sydney Harbour in the background.

Dave decided it was best to do this at night to disguise the view as much as possible. We had four hours to kill, so we made it back to the bar in Sultanahmet, ordered a few beers and a water pipe and caught up on what he'd been doing at the Olympics. Tiredness got the better of our good judgment, and by the time it was dark we were quite inebriated. Nevertheless, we found a rooftop and set up the scene. I had the piece memorised and we gave it a go. We had to shoot between the calls to prayer that sang out from the dozens of mosques in the district, and I had to stand at an odd angle to block out a medieval tower.

It was hilarious, but I thought we had done a good job. The Sea of Marmara glittered out of focus in the background, doing a great impression of Sydney Harbour. Dan, our producer, agreed – in that it was one of the funniest things he'd seen. The image swam in and out of focus and, wobbling slightly, I delivered my slurred lines. He didn't agree about it being a great job, however, and we ended up finishing the episode with a voice over. A pity, in my opinion.

*

One of the aspects of *Who's Been Sleeping* that drew me to the project in the first place was that we told the stories of ordinary people, the challenges they've faced, the heartbreak, joys ... the ups and downs of normal life. So much of history is preoccupied with recounting the lives of kings and queens, presidents and prime ministers. Of course they are interesting, because, often as not, what they did affected the course of history and the lives of everyone. Often their stories are a study writ large of the frailty of man. Depressingly, most decisions made by these movers and shakers were at best wrong and at worst homicidally stupid. But drama and ineptitude on a colossal scale always make for a good study. Yet we believed that to tell stories of ordinary people like us would resonate with the viewing audience. And because the history we explore in the show is relatively recent, we can relate to their stories better than those of greater antiquity.

Even as an archaeologist, with the past as my playground, trying to understand the challenges faced by people a thousand, five thousand or ten thousand years ago is difficult. Not only because there is less evidence on which to base a story, but also because the people are a thousand, five thousand and ten thousand years back down the path of collective knowledge and experience. Because they have less experience and knowledge to draw on, their reactions to a challenge or their motivations cannot be easily deduced from a modern perspective.

As an example, the site I excavated in Turkey, Boncuklu Höyük, a 10,000-year-old settlement on the broad, flat Konya

Plateau of Anatolia, was like sites I had dug in the Jordan Valley. These guys had just started down the road towards farming and were having a go at living in one place rather than roaming around the landscape following tasty animals. The archaeological ruins showed that the houses were pretty primitive. Partially dug into the ground, they were oval in plan and made of roughly formed mud bricks and plaster floors. They were about six metres long and four metres wide, just enough space for a small family to huddle at one end and allow for an open fire at the other. In between these buildings was layer upon layer of rubbish. From analysis of the tiny fragments in these middens, it was discovered that they were made up of vegetation, mostly freshwater reeds, human faeces and animal bones.

Although the houses were small and basic, they were well kept. The plaster floors were frequently refreshed, with some houses having up to eighty thin layers of plaster. Even more curiously, human burials were found under these carefully maintained floors. Dispersed through the middens and in the graves was tantalising evidence of the people who built and occupied these spaces, beautifully carved beads (*boncuklu* means 'bead' in Turkish), polished stone pendants, and tools of carved animal bone and flaked obsidian.

What was absent from the archaeological record was evidence of domesticated animals or plants, as could be determined from the subtle differences that exist in the skeletons of domestic and wild animals, and in the shape and structure of the seeds and grains of wild types of food plants and their domesticated varieties.

So what does this tell us? What's the story? Well, straight off we can build a picture of a community of perhaps forty people living in small oval houses on a low hill on the edge of a large wetland. They would head out to hunt and fish, collecting reeds and wild plants. When they weren't hunting and gathering, they would be repairing their huts (what their aboveground structures looked like is unknown), making tools and personal items, and preparing and cooking food. Oh yes, and burying their nearest and dearest under the living-room floor. So far so good. But what's missing is an understanding of why they did any of this. Why build an oval house too small to be comfortable, why then surround the houses with presumably fetid-stinking middens, and why bury their dead under the floors?

We can guess, and we are expected to make guesses, based on combined observations from other sites or modern examples or ethnographic and anthropological accounts. And to a degree that provides a sufficiently clear picture to explain what we observe at sites such as Boncuklu. But we can never know, because there are non-physical variables that do not survive in the archaeological record, such as religious beliefs, superstitions and idiosyncratic traditions that defy obvious interpretation thousands of years later. Perhaps they built their homes as they did because it was the shape of the god that was briefly worshipped in that part of the Konya Plain. Perhaps burying their dead under the floors stopped them being dug up and desecrated by the wolves that roamed (and still do in winter) down from the surrounding highlands of the Bozdag and Taurus Mountains. Yes, no, maybe. And that's as good as we are going to get until new technology or startling finds change the picture.

It's fascinating, tantalising, mysterious and wonderful, but it's not particularly personal, and it's difficult to closely empathise with these people or understand their lives.

But if we are telling stories – as we do in the show – about people who lived only two, three, maybe four generations earlier, then their stories take on an immediacy. They're more relevant and accessible to the viewer because we can understand the predicaments, the decisions and the challenges that these people of the recent past faced. I think that is why this show has resonated so well with both the houses' owners and the viewers.

And I am so pleased that this is so. I must admit that when we were developing the show, we did not anticipate the emotion that our findings would provoke in the owners and actually in ourselves. There have been a few times that the owners, the crew and I have all welled up.

A house, once it's been around a while, is imbued with a lot of energy, both the prosaic physical energy that built it and the more intangible energy ascribed to it by its occupants (or former occupants). Many of the most important events in one's life occur within homes. Until very recently, most people entered and exited the world at home. Families are raised within the protective walls of the home. Birthdays and engagements and festivals of all kinds are celebrated, and grief and loneliness endured, behind closed doors. I defy anyone not to get emotional (whether happy or sad) when visiting their childhood home.

This was powerfully displayed during the filming of a beautiful house in the port suburb of Fremantle in Western Australia. The house was owned by a smart and eloquent couple, who had raised their three children there and had also invested significant amounts of time, energy and money into modernising and extending the old nineteenth-century building. As a consequence, they were very attached to their home. This attachment became a lot deeper when we brought to the house a previous resident. Ray was in his nineties at the time of filming and hadn't been back to the property for nearly seventy years – a lifetime.

Stooped over and accompanied by doting relatives, this nevertheless sprightly man walked through the front door and into his youth. He looked around with increasing wonder at the familiar spaces. He oohed and aahed at the extension to the rear, but it wasn't until he was out the back that the past came flooding in.

He stopped abruptly and slowly looked around. A ramshackle shed took up a third of the garden. I had been scratching my head about its age and origin. It was made of old timbers and looked agricultural, and there was a rumour that the house had at one point been a farm. This open-sided shed certainly fit the bill. It was just a shame that it didn't fit the facts. The day before, I had found aerial photo evidence to show that it was built much later than the house, sometime in the early 1940s. It was a real mystery until Ray stepped into the garden and said, 'I built that.'

You don't get that on 10,000-year-old sites, more's the pity.

He stood in silence looking around the garden. Lost in thought, he was momentarily unaware of me, the homeowners, the camera and sound crew. I watched his eyes. In fact, we were all rapt by this old man. Suddenly, a large tear rolled down his cheek and for a moment I felt like I was intruding. But then he smiled, walked towards the shed and inspected it with delight.

'I used to work on cars when I was young, so I built this shed so I could be out of the weather.' He pointed at the rough old timbers. 'I got those from the old Fremantle Wharf and that floor was from the Town Hall when they renovated it.'

Now I knew why it had been so difficult to date. The shed was made from recycled materials. Ray hadn't salvaged the timbers and flooring to reduce his carbon footprint or to be environmentally sustainable. He had done it because the stuff was free and had already been worked into useful shapes. His actions and billions of others like them, repeated across the world and through time, are major factors in how archaeological sites are formed.

*

It comes as a surprise to many, including archaeology students, that there are a series of complex interrelated events necessary to bring a once robust structure to its knees and then underground. One branch of archaeological research looks into the process of site formation. It's called 'taphonomy' and any good field archaeologist must understand the taphonomic processes, otherwise what they see underground will be less than half the story. Considering that a good archaeological site contains much less than half of what was ever there, you really have to gather as much as you can. So if you have ever wondered how a site is created, or if you have never wondered but your interest is now piqued, or if you don't really care but, having got this far, you are going to read to the end no matter what hurdles I throw in the way, here's a brief description of the typical taphonomic process.

Imagine a house standing alone in a large garden or in the countryside. It's double storey and made of brick and stone with timber window frames and a tiled roof. The gutters are metal and are in good order, as are the neat landscaped gardens. The old couple who always kept it in great condition die, and the house is locked up for the last time and sits vacant. Perhaps the estate is contested or there are no children, or simply no one wants the old place and it remains vacant.

Initially, little changes except for the garden, which becomes overgrown and unkempt, making the place look abandoned. This is then an invitation for people to see if there is anything worth nicking around the place. The first things to go are the tools in the shed. But then as time goes on, people break into the house and anything of value is taken. Probably disappointed, these break-and-enterers leave with a few objects. But now there is a breach in the building, maybe a door or a window, and it lets in the weather, animals and those people who aren't up for breaking into a place, but seeing as it's already open … and they may just cause mischief – graffiti the walls, break the toilets or smash the windows. And then someone lights a fire, which gets out of control, and the house is significantly damaged.

Now the weather and animals can access at many points. Also, the gutters haven't been cleaned for years and are full of rotted leaves, and soil, grass and even a small tree are growing out of them. Every time it rains, the water flows behind the gutters, coursing down the walls. Damp creeps into the internal fabric of the building. The carpets rot and moss grows across them and up the damp plaster walls. Paper and plaster start to fall away and, particularly at the seat of the fire, the timber and masonry start to collapse. Over the next couple of years, the structural integrity of the building starts to fail, and eventually the roof sags as the front wall bellies outwards and the window frames rot. Then, unseen one windy night, the roof slowly and unspectacularly falls in, pushing a part of the front wall into the garden.

At this stage, the house has been abandoned for twenty years. Now the second phase kicks in. With the roof gone the weather, plants and insects can really do their jobs, and the organic materials such as fabric and timber start to rapidly decay. The house is ruinous and it seems there is little question that whoever owns it (if indeed anyone owns it) cares if a few bricks or worked stone are removed to be used elsewhere. Maybe some of the larger roof timbers are still okay. Perhaps the tiles find a new home, the unbroken ones, anyway. The copper pipe is stripped away, as is any lead flashing.

Meanwhile, the garden has started to rise up.

I'm writing this during a short holiday to visit my old dad in Pembrokeshire in western Wales. It's autumn and I am always staggered by the amount of leaves that fall each year. They quickly rot and mulch down if left to their own devices, adding to the topsoil. Worms and other burrowing things mix this rich humus layer, fluffing it up and adding air. In the perpetually damp and mild of the autumn, mosses grow like mad among the grass and leaf litter. I have observed over the years that the ground and lawns around my father's cottage swell and grow, and now the ground level is higher than the patio and paths and looks like it's flowing over the hard surfaces. It actually seems as if the house is sinking into the ground.

So, our once two-storey house, forty years later, is now a pile of brick rubble overgrown with vegetation, and with the garden fluffing up around it, the ruin seems to be sinking beneath the green blanket.

Occasionally over the next couple of hundred years, someone will scramble over the disappearing ruins. They may pick up a piece of blue willow pattern and pop it in their pocket, because now that the ruin is old, the previously worthless piece of pottery has value.

Then one day, the last person who remembers the ruin dies or moves away, and the completely buried remains of the house drop out of sight and mind.

Of course, there are infinite combinations of factors that create an archaeological site, but most are formed by a combination of human and natural factors. It is the effect of the human factors, however, that causes the most head-scratching on archaeological digs. Nature is motiveless and has an understandable pattern, but humans, like Ray and his shed and the guys who broke into our hypothetical house, remove materials that are of high value or are useful. This alters the bias of the types of artefacts discovered on sites, directly affecting the interpretation of the finds and therefore the story. Equally confusing is the introduction of materials into a new structure that are of greater age or even in some cases great antiquity. This can, if one is not careful, really screw up the dating of a site.

Back in Fremantle, Ray went on to tell us how one day his father had walked through the back door of the house, as he always did after his shift at the docks. He had hung up his hat on the usual peg in the kitchen, next to the range, and suddenly collapsed and died on the kitchen floor. A butter box had fallen onto his father's back a week or so before, and although he had recovered, it seemed that a blood clot had formed. When he returned to the family home that day, it had shifted and it was curtains for him.

Ray's return to his old house was truly full of mixed emotions. For the current homeowners, the place that they held dear seemed even more precious, as it was a repository of stories important to others. As the current occupiers, they were more custodians than owners.

*

The houses on the show aren't chosen for emotional effect, however. It's a bit more functional to start with. Firstly, we sift through the hundreds of places that have been volunteered by their owners and sort them into geographical regions – we need a national spread for a national broadcaster. Then we look at what themes the history of the houses may fall into. Depending on the age of the property, there may be a number of different historical themes, but Australia has some subjects that crop up frequently. To make sure the show doesn't become repetitive, we try to ensure that these common themes, such as the gold rush or the First World War and mining, are not explored in every episode.

But above all, we choose houses if we have an inkling that there is a good story behind the bricks and mortar. And so far we have discovered amazing stories that are not only affecting, like Ray's example, but also important.

In the third series, we travelled to Bundaberg in Queensland to research an old Queenslander-style house. Bundaberg sits on the banks of the Burnett River, which snakes a lazy path through deep red volcanic soils and a rippling green sea of sugar cane. The dry rasping hiss of cane ruffled by tropical breezes can be heard for thousands of kilometres on north-east Australia's coastal fringe, from northern New South Wales to Cairns. But Bundy, as it's known, is the unofficial capital of Australian sugar production, and it was in the surrounding alluvial lowlands that some of the first commercial sugar plantations were established in the mid-nineteenth century.

The house we examined was intimately linked to early sugar production, as it had once stood at the entrance to one of the biggest plantations in the area and served as the plantation manager's house. But as we delved deeper into its story, and the general story of sugar in the area, things started to get dark.

Sugar cane was first grown in Australia on an industrial scale from 1862. But the fledgling industry needed labour, lots of cheap labour. There were no convicts, since transportation had ceased a generation before. White labour was seen to be too expensive and ill-suited to the back-breaking work in tropical conditions. More likely, in an industry traditionally supported on the backs of black slaves, it was seen to be beneath European labourers. So Queensland plantation owners looked to the Pacific, and in particular the island nations of Melanesia for workers.

Between 1863 and 1901, over 60,000 South Sea Islanders were transported to Queensland to work on sugar cane plantations. Called 'blackbirding', it was a practice of forced recruitment using coercion and trickery and kidnapping. Most came from Vanuatu, the Solomon Islands, Papua New Guinea, the Loyalty Islands, New Caledonia and Niue.

Given the description 'indentured labour', whatever way it's dressed up, the practice represented a coordinated and state-approved slave trade, thirty years after slavery was made illegal in the British Empire. It only ended in the early 1900s because of the introduction of restrictive immigration policies, often called the White Australia Policy, at the beginning of Australian federation. But, if anything, the prosecution of the White Australia Policy made things worse for the thousands of South Sea Islanders. Starting in 1904, forced repatriation tore mixed families apart and uprooted established communities. Many who had been born in Australia were expelled.

The Queensland government used contractors to ship the Islanders back home. But in many instances, people were off-loaded onto the nearest or most convenient island with no heed to whether they were from that island. So now there are still people on Pacific Islands who do not know where they are from. There are stories that ships returned to Queensland to pick up more Islanders too soon to have sailed to even the nearest island, and it is thought that these people were thrown into the sea.

It's a powerful and disgraceful story, another awful blight on the history of sugar and a shameful part of Queensland's past. It was told to me and the homeowners of the Bundaberg house by two elders of the local South Sea Islander community as we sat in an Islander cemetery. It is thought six hundred people are buried there. No one knows for sure, because the graves are unmarked and no records were kept. The cemetery lies outside the boundaries of the Bundaberg Cemetery; South Sea Islanders were not allowed to be buried there.

While the house had connections to this story through its association with the sugar industry, the personal stories that occurred within its walls were mercifully brighter and the current owners had made it into a beautiful family home.

This story showed the reality of the past. Sometimes it's good, but many times it's uncomfortable and confronting, and it's often more important to tell these stories.

Or is it?

*

I chose the title of this book as much for its statement about the perceived uselessness of my career choice as for its play on words. It's a feeling that lurks at the back of most archaeologists' minds, that we have chosen a pointless career. A hobby job. A dalliance of an affluent society. After all, how many archaeologists are there in Somalia or Eritrea? When was the last time an archaeologist cured something or contributed to an advancement that actually improved people's lives, other than satisfying a curiosity that, right up until you filled them in, they never even knew they had?

(Dropping the paper at breakfast, 'Looks like they've found the royal library of Ashurbanipal at last.'

'Oh good! I've been dying to know the fate of all those clay tablets.')

This had worried me early on in my career, but the trouble was I hadn't the faintest idea what I would do if I wasn't an archaeologist. So I kept going, and while archaeology has given me a fabulous life so far, it has taken until relatively recently for that annoying feeling to disappear. Instead of navel-gazing about the importance of my profession, I started thinking about the importance of the past. Because if the past is important, I'm in the clear. If not ...

Over the twenty-five years that I have been a professional archaeologist, I have dug up a lot of stuff: pottery, glass, stone tools, skeletons. Some of these artefacts have been aesthetically pleasing. Some have been important and changed our understanding of the past. Much has been a load of old rubbish. To be honest (and I admit this quietly and from behind a hand), I'm not that into artefacts. Okay, I'd love to dig up gold and jewels, crystal skulls, the odd holy grail and perhaps a lost ark of the covenant. But it's the stories we can take from artefacts that I think are of the greatest value.

What value does the past have? After all, it's already done and dusted, it's literally old hat. If we look at the past on a superficial level, it has a curio value. Ruins, castles and medieval cities are rare and quaint and interesting. They have a richness of form and texture, which enhances our experience of the world. Places like Rome and monuments such as Stonehenge provide a chronological context for our modern urban and rural landscapes. You just have to think about the billions of dollars spent every year by tourists traversing the globe to visit ruins to realise their worth.

But if you look a bit deeper, then things get really interesting. The past is the sum of everything we have done and all that we have learned up to now. What an incredible resource of knowledge that represents, or would represent if we could access it. Because I'm a hopeless romantic, I think of the past as a vast uncharted continent. We, as archaeologists, stumble around with pith helmets and our trusty trowels (or bull whips and gun ...) exploring this unmapped land for fragments of the billions of lives and events that make up what and who we are.

Societies have come and gone, inventions been made and forgotten and mistakes repeated. The Romans invented concrete 2000 years ago. They even worked out how to pour concrete under the sea. After the fall of the Roman Empire, the knowledge was lost for a thousand years! The Pantheon in Rome is still the largest non-reinforced concrete dome ever built. There is the potential of solving some of the greatest challenges facing the world by looking at the past. I find plunging across this uncharted continent – whether it's through research or excavation – immensely exciting; akin to being an explorer during the Age of Discovery.

So the past has aesthetic value and contains an enormous wealth of knowledge, but equally important, I think, is that the past is the foundation of how we regard ourselves as individuals, communities and nations. Archaeology developed in antiquity with rulers cherry-picking and appropriating stories of the past to make themselves look good. One of the last Babylonian kings, Nabonidus, had ancient temples rebuilt to more closely align himself with the great leaders of ancient Babylon. Antiquarians of the sixteenth and seventeenth centuries turned from historical texts to study the relics and ruins of the past. What initially started as an exercise in who could acquire more stuff to cram into their country houses turned into an exploration of national identity through identification of shared past experiences. Whether it's right or wrong, nations and national characters are forged from real or made-up elements of the past. The British, Australian and American national characters owe a great deal to antiquarians and historians who have created our origin stories in the post-medieval period, including, for Australians, the Ned Kelly legend.

I believe that most of this nation-building from the past is benign, but not all. Orwell saw this value of the past when he created in his book *1984* the infamous party slogan that 'who controls the past, controls the future: who controls the present controls the past'.

So the past is also important: it is the foundation of our societies. A nation's past is its common wealth. But it only has value if it survives in some way; so safeguarding and conserving it are imperative. And you don't have to take my word for it. Unfortunately, you only have to look at the destruction wrought to cultural heritage in current and past conflicts to realise what is at risk.

Examples such as the destruction of extraordinary ancient texts from the looted libraries in Timbuktu, the Buddhas of Bamiyan in Afghanistan and, most recently, the heartbreaking destruction occurring as a result of the Syrian civil war are not collateral damage – they are deliberate crimes against humanity. In Syria, the amazing covered souk of Aleppo is gone, the eleventh-century Great Mosque of Aleppo was destroyed by artillery fire, and jet fighters are bombing the spectacular twelfth-century crusader castle Crac des Chevaliers. The fourth-largest illegal trade in the world, behind drugs, guns and people, is antiquities. It is thought that the self-proclaimed Islamic State in the Levant raised a significant portion of its war chest from looted antiquities. But only part of this is revenue-raising. The bigger purpose is to inflict grievous wounds on their foes. A people scarred and brutalised by war may, given help and time, recover, but once their heritage has been destroyed it's gone forever, and that is a wound that will never heal.

The past only really has value, however, if people know about it. The more that people understand and appreciate the importance of the past, the easier it is to protect and conserve.

*

There were two TV shows that I remember watching as a child and realising were important. Both were broadcast in the

UK in the late 1970s. One was called *Connections*, written and presented by James Burke, a science historian who explored the interconnectivity of separate and seemingly accidental events, actions and innovations, which had unforeseen but important results years, decades, centuries later. Traversing the world, Burke explained how the invention of the riding stirrup led to the creation of the atomic bomb, and how the design of a Dutch ship led to the invention of plastic. It blew my eight-year-old mind, which is testament to Burke's scripting and presenting and to my parents for encouraging me to watch this kind of stuff.

And then a year later, the TV-watching world's minds were collectively blown by David Attenborough's *Life on Earth*, as it unveiled in dazzling colour the evolution of life on our planet in thirteen hours of ground-breaking television.

You might now be expecting something like 'It was then and there, with my knees red and indented from kneeling on the candlewick rug in front of the gas fire, that I decided that I would become a TV presenter', but I won't because it's not true. In fact, the thought didn't cross my mind until my involvement with the *Ned Kelly Uncovered* documentary.

But what those TV shows did fire was my interest in storytelling. I have spent my whole life immersed in stories. Every night when I was little, my dad would sit on the end of the bed and tell me fairy stories. In his measured and deep voice, he imbued in the tales an element that made them more real, more scary. It's such an enduring connection to him. He didn't have to write them. He just had to tell them the right way. That is the power of the story and the storyteller.

Then I started to read children's mysteries such as Enid Blyton's *Famous Five*, the *Lone Pine* books and Lucy Boston's *Green Knowe* stories. These gave way to Tolkien and Isaac Asimov and Ian Fleming. I loved the journey that a good story would take you on and how it would keep you up into the night, with a torch under the covers. I have always held authors in the highest esteem, and after seeing both *Connections* and *Life on Earth*, I also appreciated the importance of telling great stories well on television.

One thing I didn't appreciate at the time but realise now is that providing context is a huge part of storytelling, and of archaeology. Putting the world-changing invention of plastic into a context of connected events stretching back hundreds of years completely changed the story from being interesting to important. Explaining the evolution of the life on our earth took us from being observers of the natural world to being deep in the mix. The past gives our lives context and I certainly feel that my appreciation of it has given me a better understanding of the here and now.

In his book *The Go-Between*, LP Hartley wrote, 'The past is a foreign country: they do things differently there.' I disagree. The past isn't a foreign country, it isn't alien. It's just a story of all that we have been, the good the bad and the downright ugly. And it's a story that's far too important to be relegated to history.